Intergovernmental Mediation

About the Book and Authors

Disputes between government bodies are usually settled through either political bargaining or litigation, but a third method has been successfully utilized in Virginia. Since 1980, a number of municipal annexation disputes have been settled using formal mediation as a tool. The authors draw on their experiences in mediation and local government to explore the formal interactions of adversaries and to analyze the patterns of interpersonal exchange—the vital subjective dynamics that determine the outcome of negotiations. They discuss the important roles a third party plays by conveying and legitimating information and by supporting norms of good faith bargaining in hostile confrontations. The book clearly demonstrates the effectiveness of intergovernmental mediation as a means of resolving complex public policy issues between competing groups of government officials.

Roger Richman is professor of public administration at Old Dominion University. **Orion F. White, Jr.,** is a professor at the Center for Public Administration and Policy, Virginia Polytechnic Institute and State University. **Michaux H. Wilkinson** is executive director of the Virginia Commission on Local Government.

Published in cooperation with
the National Institute for Dispute Resolution

Intergovernmental Mediation
Negotiations in
Local Government Disputes

Roger Richman,
Orion F. White, Jr.,
and Michaux H. Wilkinson

Westview Press / Boulder and London

Westview Special Studies in Peace, Conflict, and Conflict Resolution

Published in 1986 in the United States of America by Westview Press, Inc.; Frederick A. Praeger, Publisher; 5500 Central Avenue, Boulder, Colorado 80301

Library of Congress Cataloging-in-Publication Data
Richman, Roger.
    Intergovernmental mediation.
    (Westview special studies in peace, conflict, and
conflict resolution)
    Includes bibliographies.
    1. Annexation (County government)—Virginia.
2. Annexation (Municipal government)—Virginia.
3. Mediation—Virginia. I. White, Orion F., Jr.
II. Wilkinson, Michaux H. III. Title. IV. Series.
JS451.V65R53 1985   352'.006'09755   85-17943
ISBN 0-8133-7077-9

Printed and bound in the United States of America

The paper used in this publication meets the minimum requirements of the American National Standard for Permanence of Paper for Printed Library Materials Z39.48-1984.

6   5   4   3   2   1

Contents

Tables and Figures

Foreword

The goal of the National Institute for Dispute Resolution is to enhance the fairness, effectiveness, and efficiency of the processes through which Americans resolve disputes. One way to achieve that goal is to document innovative dispute resolution processes where they are being successfully employed. From this approach come lessons that can be assimilated and applied in other locations and under different circumstances.

The experience using mediation to resolve local government boundary disputes in Virginia is a case in point. For that reason, the institute was pleased to support the research that led to this book. In it the authors not only document how mediation was used to negotiate settlements of boundary disputes affecting several jurisdictions, they also present valuable information about the use of mediation that can be very helpful in resolving other intergovernmental disputes. In short, they depict not only particulars concerning Virginia but patterns applicable elsewhere.

For this contribution to our knowledge of the use of mediation, particularly in settling intergovernmental disputes, all those interested in advancing dispute resolution must be grateful to the authors. They have added a valuable volume to the rapidly growing dispute resolution bookshelf.

Madeline Crohn, President
National Institute for Dispute Resolution

Acknowledgments

This book could not have been written had not local government officials in Virginia accepted mediators in their disputes. To these city, town, and county officials in a dozen disputes and to the past and present members of the Virginia Commission on Local Government, we owe a primary debt of gratitude for their support for this innovation in public policy negotiation.

We thank William Drake of the National Institute for Dispute Resolution for his advice in organizing the manuscript, and we thank the institute and particularly its president, Madeline Crohn, for supporting this writing project.

We owe a debt of gratitude to Sandra Wiley, who initially edited the manuscript and brought cohesion to the writing styles of three authors; to Barbara Bingham, who typed long hours to bring forth a clean manuscript from often hardly legible drafts; to Jane Hendricks for her fine artwork; and to Susan McEachern, Kathy Streckfus, and Vicki Gundrum at Westview Press for their advice and guidance and copyediting of the final manuscript.

Roger Richman
Orion F. White, Jr.
Michaux H. Wilkinson

Introduction

In Virginia, municipal annexation of county land creates major intergovernmental conflicts. Sometimes labeled Virginia's intergovernmental wars, annexation disputes have, since 1902, been committed to specially appointed courts for trial and binding decisions.[1] These disputes pit cities and towns against their neighboring counties in what local officials see as win/lose contests involving important local fiscal and political resources. In many of these cases deeply felt value conflicts surface between city and county negotiators, compounding the impasses on the issues. Officials in one county that faced an annexation petititon, for example, recalling bloody Civil War battles in the area proposed for annexation, suggested with real feeling that they were ready to "get some old mortars and field pieces from the war museum, put 'em on the hill and shell those [city] guys if they try to cross the river."[2] This study describes the introduction and practice of formal mediation processes in these disputes.[3]

The process of mediating public policy disputes has developed around the country in unique cases; consequently there has been little continuity in mediation opportunities. Most of the major cases reported have involved special circumstances that facilitated mediator entry to the particular dispute. Mediation in most public policy disputes have been individual one-off demonstrations rather than a developed practice in a particular dispute arena within a structured context of formal public procedures for judicial and public review of negotiated settlements.[4]

This study describes a different situation; it reviews the experience gained in a five-year-old practice of formal mediation in major interjurisdictional disputes in which basic conditions of mediator entry are established by a state statute administered by a state agency. At disputing parties' request under statutory provisions, independent mediators have been appointed by the agency, the Virginia Commission on Local Government, in fourteen intergovernmental boundary dispute cases between 1980 and 1985. Settlements have been negotiated in seven of these cases to date; three cases are currently being negotiated.[5] The mediators in these cases, exposed to a comparable set of basic issues, have been able to experiment, to learn, and to generalize findings about the mediation process in intergovernmental settings.

This study has two main goals: (1) to offer description and analysis for theory building in the dynamics of intergovernmental negotiation and in the role of the mediator in intergovernmental disputes and (2) to document the statutory and administrative context and the experience of formal intergovernmental mediation in Virginia in municipal boundary disputes. Two of the authors are mediators who have developed this technique, and one is the director of the state agency that oversees the process of changing local government boundaries.

This study has six chapters. In Chapter 1 the authors present an overview of the relation of theory to practice in mediation, as well as brief synopses of the relation between structure and dynamics in interjurisdictional negotiation and of the mediation role in complex negotiation structures.

In Chapter 2 the authors describe the evolution of Virginia's new approach that applies negotiation processes to the annexation dilemma. They begin with a review of the legislative studies that resulted in the state's 1979 legislation establishing a new focus on negotiated settlements in intergovernmental boundary issues. The structural role of the new agency, the Commission on Local Government, in both the annexation process and the initiation of mediation in these disputes is described, followed by an overview of the experience using mediation in these disputes in the four years since the agency was established.

Chapters 3 and 4 are in-depth studies of the structured negotiation process employed by mediators in two annexation cases. Each case involved lengthy negotiations in a highly adversarial context between parties convinced at the outset that negotiations would likely be perfunctory and that only a court order would force their opponent to accept resolution of the issues. Each negotiation lasted for several months and dealt with complex intergovernmental issues that went well beyond the original issues in dispute.

The case studies in Chapters 3 and 4 demonstrate the effects on interjurisdictional negotiation of three critical variables: (1) the external environment of statutory requirements and decisionmaking by the administrative agency, (2) the parties' involvement with negotiating positions and with each other, and (3) the mediator's interventions in organizing the negotiations and in shaping the internal structure of a long negotiation. The mediators have found that the development of the internal order of a dispute is a prerequisite for settlement and that the development of this order in turn depends on the movement of the parties through a sequence of phases in the joint experience of the negotiation.

In Chapter 5 the authors describe the dynamics of intergovernmental negotiation. Based on their experience mediating disputes in Virginia's program, they analyze the relevance of the nonexplicit and in particular the nonrational interests involved in public sector negotiations. Chapter 5 offers a conceptualization of the sociopsychodynamics that drive negotiations and presents a model of how team strategizing and positioning develops from the internal concerns the parties hold, and affects the very substance of proposals and the interaction dynamics in the negotiation process.

The role of the mediator in intergovernmental disputes is depicted in Chapter 6. The theme of negotiation substructures and subarenas is developed, specifying the various roles of the mediator in joint negotiation sessions, in intranegotiation team meetings (caucuses), and in meetings between negotiators and their primary constituencies—their governing boards. The various structural components affecting the surface level dynamics of negotiations are reviewed here.

Chapters 3, 6, and part of Chapter 1 were written by Roger Richman, associate professor of public administration at Old Dominion University and mediator in twelve intergovernmental disputes. Chapters 4, 5, and part of Chapter 1 were written by Orion F. White, Jr., professor of public administration at Virginia Tech University and mediator in four intergovernmental disputes in Virginia. Chapter 2 was written by Michaux H. Wilkinson, who has been executive director of the Virginia Commission on Local Government since its inception.

1

Theory and Practice

In this book of theoretical and case studies we hope to help establish a new linkage between theory and practice in the field of conflict and dispute resolution. Our intention is to add to the material available for the training and continued education of effective mediators and, in doing so, to revise and expand the perspective for viewing the relation of concept to action, theory to practice, in the professions that apply social science knowledge.

The prevailing viewpoint on how theory should link to practice is founded in the modern behavioral social science approach that seeks causal explanations founded on empirical data (preferably quantified) and elaborated through logical deductive reasoning. This framework depicts the proper role of theory as the production of reliable predictions, so that those seeking to act can make valid judgments about the probable outcome of various lines of action. Predicting outcomes through analysis and then choosing actions that seem most probable to lead to desired results while avoiding negative possibilities make up what is generally regarded as the rational approach.

This scheme of rational action involves many difficulties, not the least of which is that social science knowledge—even in those fields based on quantified data and highly simplified axiomatic assumptions, such as economics—has a great deal of difficulty living up to its requirements. One response to this problem is to adopt a highly eclectic approach to theory application; the field of psychology seems to be characterized by this response. Another is to continue the attempt to find reliable explanation—even in face of highly mixed results. This response seems to be the one of choice in sociology, economics, and political science, perhaps because application of knowledge in these fields is more general and programmatic than specific and clinical.

Still another response is to eschew theory altogether and to claim instead that a given field of practice is not amenable to theoretic analysis and must be carried out ad hoc, situationally, or intuitively. Judging from a literature review on negotiation, and particularly on the role of mediation in negotiated dispute resolution, one would conclude that this last choice is the most prevalent response among practitioners and researchers in the field. Practicing mediators see dispute resolution as a highly dynamic process of deal cutting, in which the mediator exerts pressure on the parties to split the difference separating them. Relations between parties are depicted as purely adversarial; disputes are seen as sublimated war. In this view conflict resolution is rather predictable and mechanical—a matter of arriving at the right price. Mediators picture themselves as operating intuitively, by the seat of their pants; they tend to deride the idea that mediation can be explained theoretically.

This viewpoint is unfortunate, derived more from the dilemmas of behavioralism than from the nature of negotiation and mediation as phenomena. By excessively emphasizing surface-level aspects of social process, behavioralism seeks to reduce a social process like dispute resolution to only these more easily apprehensible variables. Although this approach would seem to simplify the task of explanation and prediction, it actually complicates it vastly—perhaps, indeed, making it ultimately impossible.

Our study and practice of dispute resolution strives to formulate an approach that joins deep-level institutional or structural factors with surface-level behavioral or dynamic factors. Our aim is to describe each type and suggest, at least in an implicit and preliminary way, how they interact and affect each other.

Structure and Dynamics

Perhaps one of the best ways to illustrate the concepts of structure and dynamics is by looking at group dynamics. Group facilitators are aware that the behavior of every group is fundamentally conditioned by a number of structural elements. Two of the most obvious and powerful of these are the spatial arrangements of the group members and the stages that groups experience as they proceed from formation to task performance and completion. Such elements are structural in that they operate on the behavior of group members in ways that lie beneath their conscious awareness. These deep-level structural elements are the basis for behavioral patterns in the sense that they potentiate behavior in given directions. Seating members in a circle, for example, disposes the group toward harmony and consensus, whereas a line of two chairs facing each other sets up the potential for confrontation. Similarly, definite behavior patterns characterize each of the stages that groups undergo as they develop. This process of development itself at least potentially induces the behavior.

Furthermore, the facilitator knows that certain elements will come into play through group interaction. Like the structural elements these dynamic elements push behavior in given directions. For example, the elements of accuracy and empathy in listening skills and sociometric patterns can produce states of harmony or dissension, depending on conditions. These elements are predominantly found at the surface level in the group and, therefore, can be consciously perceived by group members. These elements that group members consciously perceive increase the group interactions at the surface level since group members can respond to these elements by stopping them or changing their direction. These actions, in turn, can produce further changes in behavioral patterns.

The role of the facilitator is both defined and conditioned by these two levels of group reality. The levels define the facilitator's role in the sense that the facilitator's objective is to be aware of the power and effects of both the structural and dynamic elements and to intervene to raise the group's awareness of these so that any potentially negative effects of the elements on the group's work may be neutralized. The levels condition the facilitator's role in the sense that the structural and dynamic patterns characterizing a particular group will determine at least initially and sometimes finally the scope of the facilitator's action that the group considers legitimate. The role of the facilitator has an edge on these elements because (1) it is somewhat marginal to the group and, hence, partly out of the range of its structural and dynamic influence, and (2) it involves a deeper awareness of the laws of structure and dynamics in groups. With this leverage, the facilitator can work toward positive results.

The Contribution of This Work

An approximate likeness can be drawn between the picture we have just sketched and the process of dispute resolution. First, in intergovernmental disputes of the sort we have worked on and studied, a definite pattern of structural elements has appeared. Typically, there is an external frame, specified to a great extent by the law and by the arrangement of governmental institutions, that heavily affects the process of negotiations. In addition, those cases familiar to us have revealed a rather consistent developmental pattern, with its own logic and internal order. This developmental pattern gives the negotiation process a life of its own, with a synergistic power to produce outcomes beyond the initial intentions of each concerned party.

Second, intergovernmental disputes display a pattern of negotiation dynamics made up to a significant extent of speaking and listening dynamics, sociometric patterns, and so on, that are typical of any group process but which possess distinctive structural elements. These elements are represented at the level of dynamics in the way that they shape perceptions—namely, perceptions parties form of each other and of the mediator. Furthermore, these group dynamics are political and representational and reflect multiple, varied individual career goals. Group participants have diverse power bases that may not be consistent with their formal status, and they pursue various objectives according to the needs and wishes of their supporters while attempting to further their own varied career objectives. (In an organizational setting, the degree to which these characteristics applies varies.)

Third, the role of the mediator in intergovernmental disputes must be defined within the constraints set by these structural and dynamic elements. In this respect, the mediator is like a group facilitator; however, unlike the group facilitator, the mediator has an official status in the process. Because of this official status and the mediator's involvement with parties in reformulating the substance of issues, the boundaries of the mediator's role are less precise than those of the facilitator's role. Structure and dynamics interplay so heavily and closely that the rules governing the mediator's behavior are constantly changing. Sometimes the negotiation process demands that the mediator extend himself or herself beyond the intermediary role in negotiations; at other times much more distant kinds of role behavior are called for.

Under such ambiguous conditions, the mediator needs to consider such questions as: What structural factors are at work? How do they affect dynamics? How might dynamics alter perceptions of the structural factors? The answers to these questions might provide insight that will be useful to the mediator not so much in predicting the course of events but in formulating a next step in negotiations. The mediator who has a deep understanding of the negotiations process and who asks these questions can see disputing parties as much more than adversaries. Consequently, the parties can be moved from mere deal cutting toward collaborative problemsolving, in which the synergistic effects of negotiation can be obtained. In the complex and changing situation of negotiating, what to do next is the ultimate question. It cannot be answered well with conceptual tool kits that omit either structural or dynamic elements; thus, the main thrust of the studies in this book is to describe both these sets of factors and show their relation. By doing so, we hope to bring conceptualization directly into the arena of mediation practice.

The remainder of this chapter summarizes our findings by describing structural and dynamic elements at work in local government dispute negotiations and the mediation role as it emerges from our cases.

Structural Factors and Mediator Roles

The Framework of Law and Policy

The mechanisms of public policy (that is, law and administrative process) create conditions that establish adversary relationships in public sector disputes and institutions and processes (for example, mediation) to regulate and help resolve these disputes. In the disputes described in this book, the substantive issue of municipal annexation was (and in a sense still is) framed by statute as an adversarial process to be settled through judicial proceedings. This design resulted in very few negotiated settlements in annexation cases in Virginia in the seventy-five years that preceded the 1979 amendments to the state's annexation laws. In 1979 the legislature modified the statute by adding new procedures for both state agency administrative review and negotiation and mediation, while retaining the judiciary's decisionmaking role. Since the modifications, most annexation cases have been settled through negotiations.

The new statute called for the creation of a state agency to regulate annexation and directed the state agency to advocate negotiation as an alternative to litigation. That agency, the Virginia Commission on Local Government, has actively supported negotiations and the appointment of mediators in them, raising the possibility that local officials could negotiate in a policy area they had previously relegated to the adversary process. Thus the annexation process in the state has been transformed from one in which litigation predominated to one in which negotiated settlements are the norm. The advocacy of negotiations has encouraged local government officials expert in the local equities of annexation cases to craft their own settlements to these contentious issues.

As well as conditioning the external structure of disputes, laws indirectly influence the internal structure and dynamics of intergovernmental negotiations. The parties, of course, directly engage one another throughout the negotiations—in deciding to continue to negotiate, to make concessions, or to stand firm and prepare to leave the process. They also separately engage in a self-directed analysis about alternatives under the structure of law and policy. Negotiators continually test their alternatives to negotiation; they measure offers made and received against their conjecture of what litigation would yield. They do not, in most cases, objectify the odds of losing their cases; negotiators are predisposed to assume that the courts will support their position.

One of the primary roles of mediators is to clarify parties' options for either remaining in negotiations or pursuing litigation or delay. Parties in public disputes negotiate while testing (hypothetically) their alternatives to negotiation; therefore, mediators frequently review with these parties past decisions and clarify the influence of law and policy on the case, which helps the parties examine factors influencing their willingness to engage actively in the negotiation.

Mediators also help parties interpret the framework of law and policy because settlement concepts must be developed within the limits of existing policy as interpreted by both the designated state agency and by the special annexation court. Furthermore, our case experience indicates that a successful settlement system must be specially crafted to the statutory and administrative framework regulating the particular policy area. At the operational level, disputing parties must come to see, among other things, that a policy choice is available and that a negotiated settlement can be developed—that the statute regulating the subject enables the parties' interests to be balanced, and that the dispute resolution system does not hinder or restrict access to alternatives to negotiation—indeed it provides the possibility of relief from externally imposed decisions. In short, the parties must come to see the utility of negotiation as an alternative dispute settlement option within the given framework of law and policy.

The Evolutionary Stages of Complex Disputes

The least visible, though important, structural feature of complex negotiations that we have encountered involves what we have already noted as the autonomous nature of the negotiating process. We have seen across ten different cases a common process of negotiation unfold— an evolutionary process that seems to describe a generic pattern that animated these cases. The two case studies we present reveal that, at their foundation, negotiations have a life of their own. There is a pattern to negotiations that operates beyond the conscious control and beneath the awareness of the parties acting them out.

In our cases we have identified five phases in the negotiations process: (1) exploration and formulating of strategies; (2) formal presentation of proposals, (3) problem solving, (4) confrontation and a return to competitive bargaining, and (5) agreement seeking. These phases, which mark the evolution of the joint enterprise between negotiators in an adversarial conflict, have been drawn from our direct observation of different behavioral regularities among the negotiators at different stages in the negotiation. The behavioral patterns observed are generally consistent across a range of intergovernmental mediation cases in which the structural characteristics of the dispute are similar. The phases represent levels of the interteam development of issues and the important intrateam development of issues and levels of the approach each side takes to the negotiation. They mark the character of intrateam and interteam dynamics prevailing at any given stage in the negotiation. The phases describe how the individuals making up the negotiating teams are perceiving the negotiations as a whole—any single phase indicates the status, or state, of the negotiation at a point in time.

Our observation that negotiations do have a life of their own, governed by an underlying structural dynamic, seems to have rather profound implications. Future research on the negotiation process, for example, could well focus on furthering our understanding of this structural pattern rather than upon negotiation behaviors and the corollary matter of how to be effective at negotiating, especially in the sense of how to win.

The Organization of Negotiation

A negotiation between two parties, each of which represents a wider constituency, involves a network of linkages between separate centers of activity and decision. The decision centers in disputes between local governments, exist within (1) each negotiating team, which must develop a negotiating program; (2) each governing board, which must set an agenda and review the work of its negotiating team; and (3) the center of joint activity, which is the joint negotiating session.

These separate decision centers are linked fundamentally by the common imperative of settling the dispute. They create a set of dependent relationships with clear roles for each—for example, developing positions, approving positions, and exchanging proposals in a joint enterprise. In this sense they make up an emergent organizational form, configured about the shared temporary goal of creating a settlement.

Negotiations in complex disputes require the parties to fashion relationships that support clear communication and shared understanding of the meanings attributed to important concepts. Mediators, on entering disputes, reform communication paths among the decision centers and greatly enhance development of the negotiation as an entity. By providing a neutral, third-party role, mediators can promote the negotiation as a purposeful, goal-oriented program among independent actors operating within independent decision centers.

Mediators often focus on communications by either usurping direct communications between the parties (the model of separated parties with a shuttling mediator) or by more subtly affecting the flow of information between the parties. Mediators also deal with the extended structure of the negotiation. On entering a negotiation, they meet with the governing boards, which must ratify settlements, as well as with the negotiating teams. Mediators may meet with elected officials individually or in groups. Mediators are called upon to orchestrate several settings in the negotiation: (1) They may be required to meet frequently with individual officials one-on-one, (2) they meet with each of the governing boards at separate times, (3) they work intensively with the two negotiating teams selected by the governing boards, and (4) they attend and facilitate the joint negotiating sessions. Through the continuous selection and combination of these activities, mediators develop the structure of their own relationships to negotiators and they develop a structure of relationships between negotiating parties—either through their own neutral role or by facilitating direct contact between parties by meetings, phone calls, or written materials. Mediators' actions help establish and define the structural relations between the parties in a negotiation.

Negotiation Dynamics and Mediation Roles

The three structural factors just identified—external law and policy, the evolutionary phases of development within the negotiation process, and organizational relationships established in the negotiation—influence the pattern of surface level interactions, or the observable behavior we call the dynamics of negotiation. These structural factors influence negotiation processes by two complementary means: (1) through position development and (2) through interteam and interpersonal dynamics.

Strategizing and Position Development

The core of a negotiation—the development and transmission of positions on substantive issues—is almost universally accompanied by calculated strategies and tactics that parties use to try and seek to impose or gain their objectives. The strategies selected are influenced directly by parties' perception of the state of the negotiation, and this perception is constructed largely from the parties' evaluation of the three structural factors previously identified.

The selection of strategy and tactics does not, in our experience, always follow the development of negotiating positions on the issues (as they invariably would in a "rational" negotiation process). We have observed position development taking place sometimes prior to the selection of tactics, sometimes even after it, and often simultaneously with it. Parties often seem to define substantive positions in the context of the state of the negotiation.

In the local government political world that envelops intergovernmental negotiations, the frustrations of negotiators often surface in the strategy development process: negotiators select a strategy primarily as a vehicle to express their perception of the state of the dispute. In one clear example, negotiators in one case articulated a reluctance even to put together a proposal because the other team did not deserve to get one. This strategy was based not on a reading of the structural factors frame and the substantive merits of continuing to reciprocate proposals but on the opinion of several team members that their opponents were unworthy of sufficient regard even to be considered a negotiating partner.

Enactment of adversarial strategies and tactics by each party is a routine feature of negotiations. Mediators attempt to participate in strategies and tactics by being present during their formulation (when the parties permit) and their execution. If mediators are present in strategy formulation sessions, they may be able to contribute to the parties' discussions and strategies. Negotiators in adversarial disputes will typically design their strategies (defensive or offensive) based on a sense of their power—that is, the extent to which they are able to manipulate and control information to their advantage. Negotiators are always surprised when their strategies backfire—when the other team reacts negatively to attempts to force them to play by another's rules. Mediators, working on strategy formulation with the parties, are sometimes able to make the negotiators appreciate the effect their strategy would have by suggesting the negotiators consider their own reactions if it were deployed on themselves. Mediators can help the parties to eliminate the most negative, emotionally charged conditions of their strategies.

Mediators may, on occasion, intervene in the deployment of strategies designed to manipulate information essential to the successful implementation of a settlement. At the surface level of interactions in negotiating sessions, mediators often need to intervene in the deployment of a strategy if it is creating heightened emotions and, consequently, negative exchanges between the parties.

Strategy formulation and position development—the phenomena of explicit calculation of issues and offers—in our view owes less to cool, analytical evaluation than to the negotiators' own mediation of their vital interests. The three structural factors described above serve as the vehicle by which the negotiators perceive the state of the negotiation. All the structural factors, particularly organizational relationships among the parties and the mediator, are susceptible to restructuring through mediator interventions.

Sociopsychological Dynamics and Mediator Roles

Although negotiation is portrayed by participants as a rational, even cool, calculation of positions, the roots of negotiation behavior lie in nonrational vital interests and wants of individuals. This is the greatest paradox of negotiations: Even though parties attempt to rationally calculate negotiating positions, they become caught up in expressing nonrational vital interests that, in turn, become part of the reality, the substance, of the negotiation. In fact, the explicitly rational calculation of positions and their conveyance through carefully orchestrated strategies and tactics turn out to be driven by individuals' internal vital interests and wants. These internal psychological requirements sometimes are well concealed, but they gain form in both the development of positions for negotiation and in the interpersonal dynamics of the negotiation.

In Chapter 5 we put forward a conceptual model of negotiation dynamics in which the development and communication of negotiating positions are seen as products of the interaction of psychological requirements and social forms with the substantive issues of the negotiation. A three-stage model of position development is described in which negotiators establish an initial bottom line (Position I); develop offers conceding much less than the bottom line, to be able to horse-trade (Position II); and through the dynamics of negotiation, actually convey yet a third position (Position III). Each position is affected by individuals' vital interests. The bottom line (Position I), for example, reflects not only the least the negotiators could settle for as an alternative to impasse but also functions as a psychological bottom line—that is, as a base for individual negotiators to identify what they must have to feel they have won or not lost the negotiation and a base for the social process of solidifying the members of the negotiating team, establishing its identity, drawing it together as a unit. Although Position II may be agreed upon by the negotiators as the position on the issues they intend to convey to the other side, the act of conveying Position II involves its translation into yet another position, Position III—what is actually conveyed and heard. Different communication formats and different negotiator styles affect the meanings attributed to the position; in the process of communication the substance of the position received often differs from that initially intended. A rich environment of meanings conveyed and received and of interpersonal dynamics is found throughout the negotiations, in joint sessions and in caucuses.

Mediators can be very active at the surface level of negotiations in which interpersonal events comprising negotiation dynamics are communicated between parties. A great deal happens at this level, and a major responsibility of the mediator is to be consciously aware of these dynamics and to track the effects of them as much as possible.

An effective mediator can help with the management of emotion by making the participants more aware of the effect language and tone have on feelings. When the parties are discussing the issues of a dispute, they frequently employ language they think is completely innocuous that, in fact, is quite harmful and can inflame the emotions of the other team. In one case, for example, county team members frequently referred in the coolest, most innocent and objective tone to their desire to protect a particular area of land from annexation. The city team visibly rankled at the word "protect" because they read into it a variety of negative implications about city government. (Admittedly, the county believed some of these implications to be true, but they were unaware of all the implications; the point is that constantly stimulating and restimulating such reactions on the city's side impeded the talks.)

Another aspect of negotiational dynamics that often requires assistance by mediators is the efficiency of listening and its corollary issue, semantic tangles. As organizational research has amply documented, the efficiency factor even in work-related (hence important) communication is astoundingly low, and this is as true for communications in negotiation meetings as it is for work related communications. Sometimes parties simply do not hear each other, at other times they misunderstand; seldom are they able to communicate their messages as intended. At a key point in one negotiation, the mediator interrupted a participant who was just beginning to respond to a statement from the other side and asked him to tell the other team what he understood to have just been said. Perplexed, he blurted out, "I don't have the slightest idea what they just said!"

Those who participated in the case studies in this book note that one of the mediator's early moves may be to establish a set of norms, ground rules, or negotiating conventions as a framework for the talks. Establishing these norms is one of the more important things that the mediator can do to improve the dynamics of negotiations. In representing these norms, the mediator presents himself or herself as the authority figure who defines appropriate behavior. This assertion is important more at the symbolic level than in actual practice because no mediator would get very far in actually issuing fiats about the behavior of the negotiators. But the simple presence of the mediator places the talks in the broader settings of society and government in general, where reasoned discourse and fairness are broadly accepted norms. Furthermore, the mediator represents a norm of positive strategy formation, that is, formation of strategies concerned with how to achieve settlement. The mediator is a counterweight to the tendency of parties in dispute to skew discussions toward extreme positions. To the parties, the mediator must symbolize moderation and balance.

The Mediator in Action

Mediators are fixers. Their role provides communication channels apart from the parties' occasionally too hot or too cool communications, and their interventions are designed to alter perceptions and actions both on substantive issues and on noncognitive structures and dynamics affecting the negotiating relationship. What guides the mediator in action? What theories of mediation practice exist? What is the role of theory when the mediator is inside a case and action is required?

Our approach to mediation theory focuses on the nature of the structural and dynamic factors and their interaction as a mutual social reality is constructed by the parties in dispute. We have described our experience where structural patterns (for example, variations in the external frame of law and policy regulating dispute arenas) and dispute dynamics (intrateam and interteam group processes) combine to create the state of a dispute.

Mediators should have as much understanding as possible about these factors, and to this end, they can develop their expertise in three areas: (1) the external frame of law and policy affecting the dispute, particularly settlement conditions and outcomes of relevant previous negotiations; (2) the underlying and hidden structure of the settlement process—that is, the stages in the dispute settlement process and the implications of those stages in the dynamics of the parties' interactions; and (3) the dynamics of small group interactions, particularly the interplay of structural factors and small group dynamics in adversarial situations, as well as skills development in facilitating group processes toward action.

Knowledge of these three subject areas is essential for the mediation practitioner in public disputes. We have found that an individual's development of a repertoire of intervention techniques in substantive issues and in group facilitation skills evolves from the individual's own mediation experience and observations of skilled practitioners. But a repertoire of intervention techniques is only a foundation for a successful practitioner.

In mediation more than in other situations where the practitioner dominates the professional-client relationship and thus prescribes courses of action (law and medicine are the prototypes), the practitioner (mediator) is the servant of the parties' configuration of the state of the dispute.[1] Mediation practice, then, is particularly dependent on the setting; the mediator must be prepared to respond to the situation as it presents itself.

Earlier, we defined the essential problem of practice as "what to do next?" In mediation, the appropriate theory guiding intervention is one of action in which the practitioner regards himself or herself as engaged in a dialogue with the dispute situation.[2] We believe that mediators can cultivate a knowledge of subject matter, process skills, and a repertoire of intervention techniques, in part from observation and prior experience of their application in previous settings, and can develop a sense, an art, of how to apply these in new dispute settings. The art of the mediation practitioner, we feel, lies in the ability to engage disputants in dialogues about the situation—for example, conversations about their vital interests (as opposed to their negotiation positions), their intrateam (conscious or hidden) and interteam processes, and the ways in which their strategies and tactics are affecting the negotiation. Proceeding in this way, the mediator does not, a priori, take a high-profile position upon entering a negotiation. (In some cases the mediator may elect to take a high-profile position; in our judgment this position should be assumed carefully and deliberately, after interviews with the parties and an assessment of the unique circumstances of the dispute at hand.)

The mediator's position and actions both entering and during a negotiation should be based on the parties' feedback and should not be imposed. The mediator should be listening not only for the nuances in negotiating positions but for the parties' understandings of their own relation to the negotiation. In short, we have found from our practice in complex dispute negotiations where settlements involve teams of government officials that it is important for the mediator to aid the parties' understanding of the dispute situation as well as the development of formal positions on the issues. Even though the neutral role is a powerful addition to dispute situations, we have found that mediator success is predicated less on a reliance on that role than on the ability to act intuitively in bringing to bear special knowledge and skills at particular points in the negotiations.

2

The Commission on
Local Government:
A New Approach to an Old Dilemma

Few public concerns in Virginia excite a reaction equal to that engendered by municipal boundary expansions. The intensity of this reaction is caused in large part by the commonwealth's unique independent city system. Unlike those in any other U.S. state, all cities in Virginia are independent political entities whose boundaries demark a complete geographic and governmental separation from adjoining counties.[1] No county authority or taxing power extends within the boundaries of any of Virginia's forty-one cities.

Even though this system of city-county separation has major benefits (for example, the avoidance of overlapping layers of government, clear lines of political accountability, and unambiguous administrative responsibility), it creates extraordinary confrontations, when cities seek to grow by annexation. When city annexations occur in Virginia, the affected county is reduced in area, population, and fiscal resources. As a result, city annexations in the commonwealth generally encounter not only the usual citizen opposition based on hostility to higher municipal taxes but also the vehement opposition of the county government.

Virginia's independent city system not only affects the relationship between the commonwealth's cities and counties, it also conditions town-country relations. Although Virginia's 188 towns, unlike the state's cities, remain parts of the counties, with town residents supporting both governments with their taxes and voting for officials of both political subdivisions, most towns in the commonwealth retain the legal prerogative to seek city status. Even though the requirements for city status were increased by legislative action in 1979, most Virginia towns remain eligible for city status when they attain a population of 5,000 persons.[2]

Although town annexations do not reduce a county in area and population or adversely affect in any major way its fiscal base, town growth is a cause of concern to the parent county.[3] Annexations by

17

towns of less than 5,000 persons bring those municipalities closer to the population threshold at which they become eligible for city status, whereas annexations by towns with populations already in excess of 5,000 persons add to the prospective adverse impact that the parent county will experience should such a town opt to seek city status.[4] Hence, Virginia's independent city system intensifies the reaction of counties in virtually all annexation issues, not merely those in which the annexing municipality is a city.

Another circumstance that is relevant to this study is the fact that municipal annexations in Virginia are ultimately resolved by the courts on the basis of statutorily prescribed criteria and not by popular referendum or by unilateral municipal discretion.[5] The Virginia system for determining annexation issues creates a certain equilibrium among the parties and gives the process a flexibility that is absent in other systems.[6]

Virginia initiated use of the judicial system to resolve annexation issues in the early years of this century, pursuant to a provision in the constitution adopted in 1902. That provision directed the state's legislature, the General Assembly of Virginia, to provide by general law for the extension and contraction of municipal boundaries and stated that "no special act for such purpose shall be valid" (Va. Constitution, 1902, Art. VIII, Sec. 126). In accordance with the new constitutional mandate, the General Assembly in 1904 added legislation calling for court determination of annexation issues based on the "necessity for or expediency" of each (Va. Acts, 1904, Ch. 99). The process was changed in its particulars many times in ensuing years, but it retained its basic features for over seven decades. The survival of the system should not be interpreted to mean, however, that it has enjoyed unqualified acceptance in Virginia. Indeed, the General Assembly debate when the legislation was adopted in 1904 revealed fundamental opposition to the use of the judiciary in the resolution of annexation issues and significant sentiment in favor of the use of referendum. Furthermore, within two years of its enactment the new legislation was being challenged unsuccessfully before the Virginia Supreme Court of Appeals by a county contending that the measure bestowed legislative authority upon the judiciary contrary to the constitutional requirement for the separation of governmental powers.[7]

Despite almost omnipresent opposition to the annexation process in Virginia, the process has survived and municipalities have used its provisions considerably through the years. From 1904 to the mid-1970s, approximately 120 city annexation petitions were presented to the courts for consideration; 105 of those efforts resulted in a court-decreed municipal boundary expansion. An examination of the record, however, reveals that 13 of the 15 unsuccessful city annexation actions occurred after 1950, suggesting increasing difficulty with the process since mid-century.[8]

Due to various reasons and concerns, the annexation process and the laws governing interlocal relations generally in the commonwealth have been under almost constant legislative scrutiny and review since 1950. Since that time there have been no less than six major comprehensive studies and numerous more limited ones focused on those matters.[9] A number of factors and conditions prompted this almost continuous legislative review and several merit attention here.

First, the surge of growth in Virginia following World War II resulted in the rapid development and urbanization of numerous counties and a consequent transformation of their governments. This newly found need to serve urban populations resulted in the state's legislature bestowing upon counties legal authority for the provision of services that was virtually coterminous with that of municipalities. Based upon this authority, urbanizing counties proceeded to construct facilities and extend services to meet the needs of their residents. This situation not only removed one of the traditional purposes of annexation but also eroded the popular support for the process.

Second, since a county's public facilities (for example, utilities, schools, fire stations) were generally concentrated in its urbanized areas adjacent to municipalities and vulnerable to annexation, county opposition to annexation became more vigorous. Because facilities in such areas often served residents in outlying portions of the county, their loss by annexation was often disruptive to county operations generally.

Third, many Virginia municipalities, as others throughout the nation, experienced in the post–World War II era a significant out-migration of young and upwardly mobile families and an influx of persons in search of employment and in need of subsidized housing and public transportation. These migratory patterns often created cities and suburbs with distinctly different population profiles. Such variances in population profiles often increased the opposition of suburbs to municipal annexation.[10] The aggregate effect of these and other factors was that annexation suits in Virginia were becoming extremely bitter, protracted, and costly.[11]

The Commission on City-County Relationships: Reexamining Virginia's Local Governmental Arrangements

The threat of another major interlocal confrontation over annexation in the Richmond metropolitan area in 1971 resulted in the General Assembly's establishing a new legislative study group, the Commission on City-County Relationships, and charging that body with undertaking a further review of the state's annexation process.[12] This study, however, was to go far beyond the annexation question and reexamine some of Virginia's most fundamental governmental arrangements. The law establishing the Commission on City-County Relationships (Va. Acts, 1971, Ch. 234) directed that study group to consider:

1. Whether annexation is the appropriate technique to use for the addition of territory to cities and towns, and, if not, what techniques are available and might be employed
2. What changes in the annexation statues should be made and with what purpose in mind
3. Whether counties should be given the right to become incorporated as cities as they attain certain characteristics, and by what method and criteria such characteristics should be evaluated
4. Whether the system of independent cities which exists in this Commonwealth should be modified or abolished and, if so, how such could be accomplished

The study by the Commission on City-County Relationships was the most probing and comprehensive reexamination of Virginia's local governmental arrangements and interlocal relations that had been undertaken for decades. When the commission submitted its final report to the governor and General Assembly in 1975, it noted the breadth of its review and the complexity of the issues it had considered. The commission's 1975 report properly observed that there were "few aspects of local government and public policy" in Virginia that were unaffected by the questions it had considered.[13]

The commission's report endorsed a number of fundamental principles that future legislation reflected (it would be several years before any major legislation would be enacted that effected any significant changes in the law governing the structure of Virginia's political subdivisions and interlocal relations in the commonwealth). First, the commission asserted its judgment that the state had a responsibility for the well-being of its local governments. With respect to this point, the commission's report noted that because the state bore "the ultimate constitutional responsibility" for local government it was obliged "to guide and assist the development of its political subdivisions" (p. 10). Recognition of this principle, the commission insisted, required affirmative action by the state to assure the general social and economic health of its localities. Indeed, the pragmatic consequences of neglecting such a responsibility would, the commission contended, ultimately affect the viability of the state itself.

Acceptance and application of this principle of state responsibility for the well-being of its local governments led logically to the commission's endorsement of an annexation process that would assure an objective analysis of relevant factors and would result in resolutions protecting and preserving the viability of the affected local governments. Since annexation questions involved consideration of technical concerns and had ramifications affecting more than local interests, it was important, the commission insisted, that "the mechanism devised for evaluating them be competent to deal with complex issues and capable of considering interests which extended beyond the immediate localities" (p. 33). The commission expressly rejected proposals for the use of referendums in annexation actions, noting that referendums afforded little opportunity for an objective analysis of technical concerns and, furthermore, constituted a "relinquishment of state responsibility" (p. 33).

It is significant to note the commission also considered proposals to create an expert administrative body to review and decide annexation issues. However, the commission was unconvinced that such a body was needed in the commonwealth and noted that although it could bring "needed experience, expertise, and consistency" to the analysis of boundary change issues, with certain proposed modifications the judicial process remained "the appropriate mechanism" for the resolution of annexation questions" (p. 34).

One of the modifications that the commission proposed was a concept that would preclude annexation in portions of the state (this was the first time such a concept was proposed in Virginia). The commission recommended that certain qualifying counties be immunized from further territorial encroachment. This immunity, which was to be founded upon a county's level of development and its provision of urban services, would protect qualifying counties from both city-initiated annexation and establishment of new cities within their boundaries.[14] In support of the proposed concept of immunity, the commission observed that "certain counties in the state govern predominantly urban populations and provide for the delivery of a full array of urban services" and, therefore, municipal governance of such areas was not required for public service purposes (pp. 29-30). Hence, the trauma of city annexation and city incorporation could safely be terminated in such areas.

Recognizing that such grants of county immunity would terminate the annexation authority of some of the state's cities, particularly its older core municipalities, and thereby remove a means of their economic growth, the commission contended that the state would be obliged "to provide fiscal remedies that will sufficiently ensure" the continued existence of such cities as strong and viable units of government (p. 28). The recommendation called for increased state financial aid to cities that lost their annexation authority as a result of grants of county immunity, reflecting again the commission's insistence that the state had an unremitting responsibility for the viability of its local governments.[15]

Finally, and most significantly, the commission refused to recommend the abandonment of the independent city system. Although the commission was fully cognizant of the pervasive difficulties that the system had created with respect to city incorporation and boundary change issues, it was also aware of the beneficial aspects of the system and the formidable problems associated with terminating it. On these various points the commission's report noted:

> The governmental simplicity, the ability to focus responsibility, and the capacity for local initiative that mark the Virginia system speak well for the continuance of city-county separation. Besides the definite positive features of city-county separation, the Commission has been mindful of the immense legal, political, and administrative problems which would result from ending the system of separation. Issues of the redistribution of general governmental powers and responsibilites, voting rights, taxing authority, and debt restriction would raise enormous difficulty upon the termination of city-county separation (p. 49).

Even though the commission recommended the continuance of the independent city system, it proposed that the state establish more stringent criteria for the creation of new cities and that the commonwealth exercise greater surveillance in the process by which they were created. To accomplish these objectives, the commission recommended that any proposed creation of a new, independent city, whether from the transition of towns or counties to city status or from governmental consolidations, be subjected to judicial review. The criteria proposed for judicial review would vary with the type (transition or consolidation) of issue presented. But in each instance review would focus largely upon (1) the capacity of the proposed new city to function as an independent municipal corporation, (2) the effect of the proposed incorporation on adjoining localities, and (3) the state's interest in preserving the viability of its political subdivisions in the area (see pp. 48-68 of the commission's report). These various recommendations proposed for the first time that qualifying counties be permitted under general law to obtain city status and that all proposals for establishing new cities be subjected to critical judicial review.[16]

In summary, after extended review of the state's local boundary change and governmental transition law, the commission submitted its final report in 1975 to the governor and General Assembly. The report's recommendations (1) reaffirmed the state's responsibility for the health and viability of the commonwealth's local governments, (2) urged continued use of the judicial system for the resolution of annexation issues, (3) endorsed the concept of immunizing qualifying urban counties from city-initiated annexation and the incorporation of new cities, and (4) proposed continuation of the independent city system concurrently with more stringent requirements governing the establishment of new cities and a critical judicial scrutiny of each proposed incorporation. Even though no comprehensive legislation on these issues was enacted for a number of years, the recommendations of the commission had a significant and pervasive impact on subsequent legislative action.

Not until its 1977 session did the General Assembly give intensive legislative consideration to the commission's proposals.[17] That year the legislature focused a great deal of its collective energy on House Bill 855 (HB855), which contained the bulk of the commission's recommendations, and on a companion measure designed to increase state aid to cities, principally those confronting major urban problems and those subject to losing their annexation options as a result of prospective grants of immunity to the urban counties adjoining them.[18] HB855 encompassed the major features and principles of the commission's 1975 recommendations, but included elements emanating from legislative review during the ensuing two-year period. Perhaps the most salient concept added to the bill by legislative action was one that would permit any city with constricted annexation authority to require the adjacent immunized county to enter into an economic growth-sharing arrangement. Under such an arrangement, the county would be required to share a portion of its growth in real estate and sales tax revenue with the city on the basis of a formula prescribed by law.[19] During the 1977 session HB855 passed the House of Delegates by a wide margin, however, it was defeated in a very close vote in the state senate. Those legislators who opposed the bill represented (1) cities contiguous to counties likely to obtain immunity under the new law, (2) counties objecting to the mandatory economic growth-sharing provision, and (3) other areas of the state with general objections to the retention of the judicial system for the resolution of annexation issues.

The defeat of HB855, coupled with the pending expiration on July 1, 1977, of the various moratoriums that had held city annexations and the incorporation of new cities in abeyance since the early 1970s, would mean that as of July of that year the state would likely experience a siege of new annexation and city incorporation actions under the old statutory provisions. Even in instances where cities had little interest in an immediate annexation, or where towns and counties had only a modest interest in city status, the fear that future changes in the law might either preclude such actions or render them more difficult could prompt precipitous annexation and transition actions.[20] Given this situation, after HB855 was defeated, the legislature in the closing hours of the 1977 session pushed through a bill that extended the moratoriums on city-initiated annexations and on the incorporation of new cities for an additional ten-year period, or until July 1, 1987.

The passage of this bill presented the governor with a major dilemma. The governor privately expressed the view that extending the moratorium on city annexations from its original establishment in 1971 through 1987 was too severe a measure. However, he too recognized that with the defeat of HB855 his veto of this moratorium extension might subject the state to a flood of annexation and local government transition actions that could be traumatic for the commonwealth. The bill extending the existing moratoriums was the subject of intensive gubernatorial consideration and was one of the last legislative measures to be signed by the governor following the 1977 legislative session.

In signing the legislation extending the moratoriums, the governor extracted from the state's two local government associations—the Virginia Municipal League (VML) and the Virginia Association of Counties (VACO)—a commitment that the impasse over the proposed comprehensive revision of the state's annexation and local government transition laws would be resolved in the immediate future and that the moratoriums on such actions would be ended as soon as possible. Some months after the close of the 1977 legislative session, VACO's executive director reported a discussion that he and other officials held with the governor during the last day for gubernatorial approval of bills:

> The Governor opened the meeting by stating that he felt that moratorium of ten years on annexation, etc., would delay the growth and development of the Commonwealth's municipalities far too long. Thus, he was inclined to veto the bill leaving no moratorium. The Association's response was that it has originally requested a moratorium extension of two years, and that it was surprised that the moratorium was extended to ten years. Considerable discussion followed and ultimately it was agreed that a joint Task-Force on Annexation, etc., would be recommended to the Association's Executive Board and to the Virginia Municipal League to work together to try to develop acceptable solutions to the relationships between counties and municipalities and to get the ten year moratorium changed to two years at the next session of the General Assembly. The Governor gave no clues to his action, but later in the day signed the bill into law.[21]

Consistent with this understanding, VACO and VML contingents met separately throughout the latter months of 1977 to develop the proposals that each would advance to end the legislative impasse. Early in 1978 these two contingents met jointly and fashioned an agreement on various outstanding issues. This agreement was formally presented to the General Assembly in February 1978.[22] The agreement contained a total of twenty-one provisions. Only a few of these provisions, however, proposed fundamental changes in HB855, the legislation defeated in 1977. Two such provisions require comment in this study.

First, the VML-VACO agreement enlarged the concept of immunity from that presented in HB855. Whereas the previous legislation would have made immunity available only to the state's highly populated and urbanized counties, the VML-VACO agreement recommended that any county be permitted to seek immunity for selected portions of its area upon satisfying the court that certain statutorily prescribed conditions were met, principally that the county was providing appropriate urban-type services in the area for which it sought immunity.[23] This provision would for the first time in the history of the commonwealth give every Virginia county an opportunity to protect certain areas from loss through annexation or city incorporation by providing a full array of urban services and by meeting other statutory requirements.[24]

Second, the VML-VACO agreement proposed the creation of a Commission on Local Government, which would be given a major responsibility for the resolution of interlocal issues in the state. The VML-VACO agreement stated that "there should be created a State Commission on Local Government through which a continuing body of knowledge about local government economic and space needs could be developed. The Commission should be a group which has the capacity to develop annexation expertise."

Not surprisingly, the VML-VACO recommendations submitted to the legislature in 1978 lacked specificity on a number of points, including the functioning of the Commission on Local Government. The two associations evidently envisioned that body as having a broad role in interlocal issues and serving in more than a fact-finding capacity. Addressing the role of this proposed commission, the VML-VACO agreement suggested, "Immunity, annexation and transition should not be automatic (except where otherwise provided by law), but alternative arrangements should be openly discussed by all affected parties before the CLG [Commission on Local Government]." Thus, VML and VACO proposed a body with dual but interrelated responsibilities: (1) the provision of technical analyses in the resolution of interlocal issues and (2) service to the parties as a medium for the discussion of alternative solutions.

The VML-VACO proposals to end the legislative impasse represented a significant accomplishment—the development of an accord on extremely volatile issues effected by representatives of the state's localities. In a prologue to their recommendations presented to the legislature in February 1978, VML and VACO proclaimed that they were "very proud of the many points" in the agreement and that it was "difficult to exaggerate the importance of finally obtaining some consensus" among local governments on these vital and difficult issues.

HB855, which was defeated in the state senate in 1977, was reintroduced in the early days of the 1978 session bearing a new designation (HB603) and was referred to a committee of the House of Delegates. Subsequent to receipt of the VML-VACO recommendations, the committee agreed to amend HB603 to include most of the principal recommendations proffered by VML and VACO, including those permitting any county to seek immunity for a portion of its territory (commonly referred to as partial immunity) and calling for the creation of a Commission on Local Government.[25] The bill passed the House of Delegates in 1978 and, following further amendment that did not seriously affect the features previously discussed, was approved by the senate the following year and signed into law by the governor on February 28, 1979. Major provisions in the legislation were not to take effect until July 1, 1980, however. The new legislation specified that the moratoriums on city-initiated annexation and on the incorporation of new cities would not terminate until that date and that no actions for county immunity would be authorized prior to then.[26]

The Commission on Local Government: Structure and Responsibilities

The legislation establishing the Commission on Local Government called for the creation of a five-member body, with members appointed by the governor subject to confirmation by the General Assembly. The legislation required that each member be "qualified by knowledge and experience in local government" and forbade membership to any person concurrently holding any other elective or appointive public office."[27] In accordance with recommendations by VML and VACO, the commission was given responsibility as both a technical fact-finding body and a medium for the negotiation and settlement of annexation, immunity, transition, and other interlocal issues (Va. Code, Sec. 15.1-945.3 [G] [H]).

Regarding the commission's technical fact-finding responsibility, the new legislation specified that any local government seeking to annex, to incorporate as a city, or to have a portion of its territory immunized from city-initiated annexation and from the establishment of a new city must submit notification of such an intent to the commission for review before it could petition the court for approval of its proposed action. Upon receiving notice of a proposed action, the legislation directed the commission "to hold hearings, make investigations, analyze local needs and make findings of facts and recommendations" relative to the issue and to prepare a report. The commission's report, which was required to be based upon the standards and factors statutorily prescribed for consideration, was to be submitted both to the affected localities and to any court that might subsequently hear the issue.[28] The commission's report was not to be binding, but it was to be received by the court and considered as evidence in the case (Va. Code, Secs. 15.1-945.7 [B] and 15.1-1170).

Regarding the commission's mediation responsibility, the new legislation stated that one of the general powers and duties of the commission was to "serve as a mediator between local governments" (Va. Code, Sec. 15.1-945.3 [G]). In addition to this general power, the new law expressly authorized the commission to "actively seek to negotiate a settlement" of any action that had formally been referred to it for critical review. It is significant to note that the new legislative arrangement permitted the commission to mediate issues either through the use of its own members and staff or through the service of a designated, independent mediator. Recognizing the inherent tension between the commission's responsibilities (fact-finding and mediation) and the need to separate carefully the discharge of the two distinct functions, the law forbade the commission from citing in its reports any offers or statements made in negotiations. It also proscribed the introduction of such offers and statements in any subsequent court proceeding between the affected parties.[29]

These provisions bestowed upon the commission the prerogative to promote interlocal negotiations and to assist such negotiations through the provision of mediation assistance. In 1980, before the commission became involved in any major interlocal issue, the law governing the commission's role and responsibilities was amended to permit any locality that was a party to either an annexation or partial immunity action to force other affected localities to negotiate on such issues. This 1980 amendment provided that after the filing of an appropriate notice with the commission invoking this mandatory negotiation process, "[t]he affected units of government shall . . . attempt to resolve their differences relative to annexation or partial immunity, and shall keep the Commission advised of progress being made" (Va. Code, Sec. 15.1-945.7 [E]). Clearly, this provision could not guarantee successful, or even meaningful, negotiations, but it was a device by which one party could at least bring the other to the negotiating table.

As with other interlocal negotiations, the commission was authorized to mediate negotiations instituted under this 1980 legislation either through its own members and staff or through the services of a designated, independent mediator. The commission was given an oversight responsibility for the new mandatory negotiations process; it was authorized to declare negotiations terminated if, subsequent to a hearing, it found that neither party was willing to continue negotiations or that three months had elapsed with "no substantial progress" toward a settlement.[30] Once the mandatory negotiation process has been terminated, parties cannot invoke it again to force negotiation of any of the issues that had been previously negotiated through this process.

Various aspects of the 1980 amendment, it may be argued, induce localities to invoke the negotiation process that it provides. A locality can invoke the mandatory negotiation process either before or after presenting an issue to the court, and the invocation of the process automatically stays any judicial action on the issue during negotiations. Thus, the new negotiation process offers a defendant locality a way to postpone court action. Alternatively, the locality initiating an annexation or immunity issue might well be inclined to invoke the mandatory negotiation process at the commencement of the commission's review so that the process might be concluded before the time when the locality might file its annexation or immunity action with the court, thereby removing the possibility that the process could delay the court review. None of these circumstances, of course, assure bona fide and good-faith efforts at negotiation, but they are sufficient to induce parties to begin a dialogue.

Developing and Funding the Mediation Role

The members of the Commission on Local Government formally took office in January 1980 and several months later employed their executive director and first permanent staff. Mindful of the cost and divisiveness associated with resolving past annexation issues in Virginia, the commission's members and staff devoted substantial energy during the commission's formative months to considering the mediation role, particularly in light of the new authority provided by the recently enacted legislation. The commission quickly concluded that the most effective way to meet its mediation responsibility would be to rely principally on independent mediators. The agency's small staff had a number of other duties placed upon it (for example, administration, technical analyses, report writing), and the commission members themselves were not full-time state employees but served the commonwealth only on a part-time basis. Moreover, the commission had a full appreciation of the skills required for effective mediation of the intricate and volatile issues that would be within the scope of its responsibility. The commission considered it imperative that the new mediation process be initiated in

Virginia by persons trained and experienced in mediation or similar conflict resolution activity.

In terms of identifying prospective mediators, the commission's executive director proceeded on the assumption that no attorney, consultant, or other individual who had ever been a known participant in any previous annexation or similar interlocal issue would be acceptable for mediation service under the new law. Individuals selected for mediation service under the new legislation, he felt, could not be "tainted" by any past work on behalf of any county, city, or town involved in these issues. Thus, the executive director did not anticipate finding prospective mediators who had any extensive or firsthand knowledge of either Virginia's annexation process or the new legislation governing interlocal relations.

Guided by this assumption, the commission's executive director focused his search on Virginia's institutions of higher learning, looking for faculty and staff who were students or practitioners of the general processes of conflict resolution. This effort identified a small cadre of prospective mediators from three of Virginia's major universities.[31] The commission's executive director did not at the outset seek to recruit a large number of mediators, preferring instead to confine the initial mediation work to a very few individuals who would thereby quickly acquire indepth experience with the substantive issues. Through a series of meetings in Richmond, these prospective mediators were introduced to the commission members so that the members could take some measure of the individuals they might designate for mediation service.

The commission's professional staff established a continuing dialogue with the mediators in the field to counsel them on the history of the annexation process, the intricacies of the new law, and other relevant concerns. By this means, the commission's staff provided substantive information to the mediators to enable them to comprehend quickly the extremely complex environment in which they were required to function. It must be stated, however, that the dialogue that developed between the commission's staff and the independent mediators focused on the law and the legal ramifications of various issues—it never involved the disclosure of the negotiation positions of the parties. Early in its operations, the commission and its staff came to understand the concern of negotiating parties that the commission be kept totally aloof from the actual negotiations. In appreciation of this concern, the commission has studiously stayed apart from the substance of interlocal negotiations being conducted under its auspices.

The statutes under which the commission operates state that the cost of independent mediation services shall be borne by the parties unless otherwise agreed (Va. Code, Sec. 15.1-945.7 [A] and [E]). The commission was determined that the cost of those services not be a bar to their use. The commission's executive director approached this concern with the expectation, perhaps without full justification, that the parties generally would be disinclined to accept outside mediation assistance and that any significant cost associated with its use would only reinforce this disinclination. Therefore, the executive director encouraged the commission to remove cost as a factor, at least initially, in any decision by a locality to use mediation services by supporting such services with its own financial resources.

The extent of the commission's financial support, if any, would be determined by the size and nature of the localities involved and by attributes of the issue. The commission did accept as a principle, however, that any financial assistance for mediation services would be contingent upon some appropriate local contribution. Such a local contribution would create, for the political subdivisions involved, a direct and tangible interest in the mediation process and a tendency to use the mediation resources economically. In some instances, the commission has borne up to 60 percent of the cost of mediation services; in other instances, where local circumstances suggested it was appropriate, the commission has left the parties to bear the entire cost.

Since deciding to invest its own resources in encouraging the use of mediation in the resolution of interlocal issues, the commission sought and obtained from the legislature funds earmarked for this purpose. In seeking funds for mediation assistance from 1982 through 1984, the commission stressed the potential savings to both the state and its localities through the avoidance of the various costs (for example, legal fees, consultants' charges, and court-related expenses) associated with protracted adversarial judicial proceedings. The commission added that because of initial skepticism about the mediation process and, in the case of some communities, a concern about cost, state aid could be a prerequisite to a locality's acceptance of mediation services.[32] The governor's office and the General Assembly have consistently supported the commission's request for funds for mediation services, granting the funds requested for 1982 through 1984, and subsequently doubling the amount available for the ensuing biennium.

Initial Case Experience

In July 1980 the commission was presented with its first major interlocal issue. That month the commission received for review an annexation action instituted by the City of Harrisonburg, which sought to annex approximately fourteen square miles of territory in Rockingham

County.[33] The commission's experience with that case was to have considerable impact on its future operations.

Upon its formal receipt of the City of Harrisonburg–Rockingham County annexation case, the commission contacted officials of the two jurisdictions and offered to assist the localities in negotiating a settlement of the issue. The county responded quickly and positively to the commission's offer, but the city's reaction was hesitant and reserved. It quickly became evident that city officials were suspicious that the county might use the commission's mediation overtures merely to delay Harrisonburg's annexation effort.[34] Since the city could not proceed with its annexation action before the court until the commission's report was submitted, Harrisonburg officials were intent upon not permitting anything to delay the issuance of that report. Responding to this concern, the commission advised the city that Harrisonburg's acceptance of mediation services and negotiations with the county need not delay either the commission's analysis of the city's proposed annexation or the submission of the commission's report on the issue. Harrisonburg officials were advised that preparations for the commission's formal hearings on the proposed annexation, due to be held several months later, could continue while negotiations were underway.

In an endeavor to encourage the city to enter negotiations with the county under the commission's auspices, a commission member visited Harrisonburg to discuss the issue with city officials. That visit was followed by a subsequent one from the commission's executive director, who was accompanied by a prospective independent mediator. These visits were to underscore the commission's strong support for the mediation process and to convince city officials that the commission would not permit that process to be used merely to delay Harrisonburg's annexation case.

Shortly after these visits, the city agreed to accept the commission's offer of mediation assistance and to pursue a negotiated settlement with the county while the commission and the two localities prepared for formal hearings on the issue. The county's acceptance of this proposed arrangement established the precedent that the commission has continued to follow: initiating interlocal negotiations with mediation assistance while concurrently preparing for a formal hearing on the issue.[35] In this manner, interlocal negotiations need not delay either the commission's formal analysis or the submission of the commission's report.

While preparing for its possible extension of mediation services to Harrisonburg and Rockingham County, the commission encountered another reason to support its decision to rely principally upon independent mediators. One attorney involved in that case questioned the capacity of the commission, or its staff, to be involved intimately in the mediation efforts and subsequently, assuming those efforts failed, to sit in judgment of the originally proposed action. The attorney argued that although the statutory proscription against the commission's citing in its report any "[o]ffers and statements made in negotiations" would prevent any written reference, this exclusionary rule would not prevent a commission member from being subtly influenced in his judgment by offers heard in negotiations (Va. Code, Sec. 15.1-945.7 [A]). For this reason the attorney was opposed to any commission member being involved in mediation efforts on any issue that the commission might subsequently be required to review in an adversarial setting. The commission did designate an independent mediator in this first case, and with only rare and limited exceptions since then, the commission has continued to provide mediation assistance through independent mediators.[36]

Negotiations between the City of Harrisonburg and Rockingham County failed to produce a settlement, so the commission was required to review critically the proposed annexation and to prepare recommendations for the court's consideration. Upon receipt of the commission's report, the city presented its annexation action to the court for ultimate disposition. Both the trial court and later the Virginia Supreme Court, which reviewed the case on appeal, endorsed the recommendations of the commission with only modest modification.[37] It may be argued that this judicial support of the commission's fact-finding role gave the agency credibility and strengthened its capacity to promote interlocal negotiations and to extend mediation services.

A second interlocal issue presented to the commission in late 1980 raised a different set of concerns and gave evidence of a distinctly different role for the commission's mediation services. Alleghany County officials requested the commission to use its good offices to promote a dialogue among Alleghany County and three adjoining jurisdictions for purposes of exploring alternative solutions to the interlocal concerns of the area.[38] Pursuant to this request, the commission met with representatives of the four localities in January 1981 to discuss the area's concerns and to determine if there was an appropriate role it might play in addressing them. As a result of that meeting, the commission, with the concurrence of the localities, designated an independent mediator to assist the four jurisdictions in exploring their mutual interlocal concerns.

The mediator and local officials from the four jurisdictions conducted a series of meetings over several months, after which all jurisdictions agreed to fund jointly a technical study that would critically examine the cost and benefits of a number of specified interlocal options including annexation, increased functional cooperation, and several forms of governmental consolidation. When the study was completed several months later, the parties resumed their negotiations by reviewing the consultant's findings and recommendations with the commission's designated mediator. This mediation effort, which extended over a three-year period, did not end in an interlocal settlement, and the jurisdictions later assumed adversarial stances before the commission as a result of an annexation suit filed by one of the jurisdictions, the City of Covington. Even so, this case demonstrated a new and distinct role for the commission's mediation services. The localities had accepted a commission-designated mediator who served initially as a facilitator to establish a dialogue and identify the issues and later as a bona fide mediator.[39]

A third major interlocal issue, which was to become a watershed experience for the new commission, was formally presented to the agency in September 1981. Spotsylvania County, the state's most rapidly growing county during the previous decade, filed notice with the commission of its intention to seek immunity for approximately twenty-seven square miles of its territory from annexation by the City of Fredericksburg and from the incorporation of new cities.[40] Shortly after receiving notice of this immunity action, the commission met with representatives of the county and the City of Fredericksburg and established a schedule for its formal review of the immunity action. With the concurrence of the parties, the commission also designated an independent mediator to assist the localities in seeking a settlement of the issue. Following intensive negotiations between the two localities, an interlocal agreement was reached and approved by the governing bodies in December 1981. That agreement constituted the first major negotiated settlement produced under the new legislation and the first generated with the assistance of a commission-designated mediator.

The state's newly established legal processes did not exempt interlocal agreements regarding annexation, immunity, and transition issues from either commission review or from the necessity for ultimate judicial sanction. Therefore, the Spotsylvania County–City of Fredericksburg agreement presented the commission for the first time with the need to review an interlocal settlement.[41] The agreement between the two localities contained, inter alia, provisions that granted the city an annexation of approximately 4.6 square miles of territory and forbade the city from either initiating or accepting an annexation of any other territory in the entire county for at least twenty-five years.[42] This latter provision became a source of considerable concern to the commission because of demographic projections indicating that well before the end of the twenty-five-year annexation moratorium included in the agreement, Spotsylvania County would have the requisite population and population density to qualify for total immunity. Thus, the agreement could foreclose forever, barring a future change in the state's immunity law, the city's prerogative to seek further growth by annexation in Spotsylvania County.

Since the City of Fredericksburg would remain a municipality of only approximately 18,000 persons following the negotiated annexation, the commission was concerned that the moratorium would prematurely restrain the growth of that city and adversely affect its future viability.

Needless to say, the commission's role in this interlocal settlement raised intricate and sensitive issues. How indulgent, probing, or assertive should the commission be in reviewing settlements of these volatile issues that had been approved by the locally elected leadership? The legislature's declared purpose in establishing the commission was to create a mechanism to help ensure that all of the commonwealth's "counties, cities and towns are maintained as viable communities in which their citizens can live," and the annexation laws of the state specifically required consideration in each annexation issue of the impact of the proposed action on the "interests of the State in promoting strong and viable units of government." Thus, there existed a statutorily established state concern for consideration during a review of these interlocal agreements (Va. Code, Secs. 15.1-945.1 and 15.1-1041 [b]). Addressing the dilemma created by this situation, the commission noted in its report on the Spotsylvania County—City of Fredericksburg agreement:

> It is evident that the General Assembly encourages interlocal negotiation and settlement of boundary change issues. Indeed, one of the legislatively prescribed responsibilities of this Commission is the mediation of these interlocal issues and the promotion of their settlement. Accordingly, the Commission concludes that its review of such interlocal settlements should be guided by a presumption of their compatibility with statutorily established standards and criteria. The Commission notes, however, that the General Assembly has elected not to exclude these interlocal settlements from its review and holds, therefore, that such presumption should not render the Commission inattentive to concerns expressed by other parties, nor render our review a pro forma endorsement of any action (pp. 6-7).

Indeed, as suggested previously, the commission did entertain reservations about the provision in the Spotsylvania County–City of Fredericksburg agreement by which the city agreed not to institute or accept further annexations involving territory in Spotsylvania County for a quarter of a century. The commission was concerned about both the legality of the long-term commitment, which would bind the hands of succeeding city councils on a fundamental governmental prerogative, and the pragmatic consequences of the lengthy moratorium. Since the legal question was an issue properly left for judicial resolution, the commission focused its review on the practical aspects of the lengthy annexation moratorium. After noting briefly the legal issue, the commission's report on the Spotsylvania County–City of Fredericksburg agreement stated:

> Whatever the answer to the legal question raised above the Commission is compelled to address the immunity issue in this report. The proposed 25-year moratorium, and the fact that it would, unlike the County's original immunity action, immunize the entire County from any further annexation by the City of Fredericksburg, will impose a rigidity on local boundaries in the area which may well be counter to the interests of the State. The Commission notes that a statutorily prescribed consideration in annexation proceedings, as well as in other interlocal issues, is the interest of the State in promoting and preserving strong and viable units of local government. The immunity provisions in this interlocal agreement may well, in actuality, grant the County complete and perpetual immunity, and totally foreclose the authority of the City to institute further annexation proceedings in Spotsylvania County. Such permanent and total foreclosure at this time cannot be found, in our judgment, consistent with the interests of the State. Without modification, the immunity provisions in the agreement impose upon the area a premature inflexibility of local boundary lines.

Based upon this concern, the commission recommended that the interlocal agreement be modified so that the city might retain a limited annexation option on territory in Spotsylvania County.[43]

The Spotsylvania County–City of Fredericksburg agreement brought two issues into focus for further legislative consideration: (1) the legality of long-term commitments by local governing bodies on annexation immunity, transition, and related issues; and (2) the propriety and desirability of having the Commission on Local Government critically review interlocal settlements. Legislative consideration of these long-term commitments became a necessity when, seven months after the June 1982 release of the commission's report on the Spotsylvania County–City of Fredericksburg agreement, a second interlocal settlement was reached between the Town of Leesburg and Loudoun County. That agreement, which contained several lengthy moratoriums on transition and immunity prerogatives, was contingent upon the removal of any legal ambiguity over the authority of local governing bodies to enter into extended commitments on these basic governmental prerogatives. The agreement stated that the settlement between the two jurisdictions would be null and void if appropriate legislation were not enacted at the 1983 session of the General Assembly that expressly authorized the long-term moratoriums included in the agreement.[44]

At the request of the governing bodies of the Town of Leesburg and Loudoun County, their legislative representatives introduced legislation before the 1983 session of the General Assembly intended to establish clearly the authority of local governing bodies to enter into such long-term moratoriums. As this measure evolved and was enacted, it not only removed any ambiguity surrounding the legality of such long-term moratoriums, but it reaffirmed the General Assembly's desire to have both the commission and the state's judiciary review interlocal agreements. The new legislation stated:

> Any county, city or town may enter voluntarily into agreement with any other county, city or town or combination thereof whereby any rights provided for its benefit in the aforementioned chapters [i.e., those chapters of the Code of Virginia regarding annexation, immunity, and local government transitions] may be modified in whole or in part, as determined by its governing body (Va. Code, Sec. 15.1-1167.1).

The 1983 enactment also expressly stated that these interlocal agreements might contain provisions for revenue and economic growth-sharing, boundary adjustments, the acquisition of real property and buildings, and the joint exercise or delegation of powers.

Any student of local government recognizes that this legislative measure bestowed upon Virginia's local governments an extraordinary grant of authority to fashion their relations with neighboring jurisdictions. The legal environment in Virginia, however, has historically been permissive in permitting local governments to construct a wide variety of interlocal arrangements. Prior to the 1983 legislation, the state's general law authorized localities to provide joint services, to collaborate in the construction and operation of public facilities, to share officers and administrators, to establish regional authorities for various public purposes (for example, parks, transportation, industrial development), to enter into economic growth-sharing plans, and to consolidate.[45] Even though the 1983 legislation was the state's first delegation of authority to local governments to waive their annexation and similar prerogatives, the General Assembly in Virginia has long given its political subdivisions great latitude in the conduct of their interlocal affairs.

The 1983 legislation, as already stated, reaffirmed the General Assembly's desire that interlocal agreements involving annexation, immunity, and transition issues be reviewed by both the Commission on Local Government and by the courts. Indeed, the new legislation directed local governing bodies to present proposed agreements to the commission for review before they are adopted. The commission is also required to conduct a hearing, undertake an analysis of each proposed agreement, and submit a report of findings and recommendations on whether "the proposed settlement is in the best interest of the Commonwealth" (Va.

Code, Sec. 15.1-1167.1). Upon receipt of the commission's report, the parties are free to adopt their agreement as originally proposed, or as modified according to the commission's recommendations, and then to submit the agreement to the court for final approval. The commission's report is not binding on the court; however, it is to be considered as evidence. The court is limited in its authority to affirming or denying the agreement, and it cannot, without the approval of the parties, modify any of its provisions.

The cases discussed here presented the commission with a variety of issues and circumstances during its formative years and required the new state agency to confront some fundamental concerns. In the aggregate, these cases had a major impact on the future activities of the commission and on interlocal relations in the commonwealth in general.

Concluding Comments

Since mid-century, local boundary change and governmental transition issues have been among the most volatile public concerns in the commonwealth. In 1980, after decades of almost continuous study, the state's legislature made numerous and major changes in the law with respect to the resolution of these issues. The changes included extending the role of the judiciary in the resolution of interlocal issues, permitting counties for the first time to initiate proceedings to protect all or a portion of their territory from city-initiated annexation, and, most notably for purposes of this study, establishing a Commission on Local Government. This commission was granted the dual responsibilities of (1) serving as a fact-finding body and aide to the court in the disposition of issues and (2) promoting interlocal negotiations and the settlement of interjurisdictional concerns.

Several salient features characterize the present legal environment in Virginia for interlocal relations. First, an equilibrium and flexibility is present in the relations between municipalities and adjoining counties because annexation and immunity issues are resolved by courts on the basis of statutorily prescribed factors, rather than by popular referendums. Second, local governments have broad authority and many options in fashioning interlocal relationships adapted to their particular needs and circumstances. Third, a mechanism (that is, the Commission on Local Government) exists to encourage and promote interlocal negotiations designed to secure locally developed settlements without adversarial proceedings. Clearly, the recent legislative enactments in Virginia have increased the opportunity for local governments to resolve among themselves their interlocal concerns. At the same time, the General Assembly has required state review and approval of interlocal settlements, a move that is consistent with the commonwealth's generally recognized and accepted consitutional responsibility for the health and viability of its local governments.

Finally, within the state's new legal environment, Virginia has seen an extraordinary array of interjurisdictional agreements, with no less than eighteen major interlocal settlements having been negotiated under the new legislation.[46] Although a narrow range of issues (basically annexation and immunity actions) initially brought the parties into negotiations, the settlements that evolved contained a diverse, rich mix of provisions. The settlements contained not only provisions sanctioning municipal boundary expansion and the immunization of specific areas, but provisions calling for economc growth-sharing, major collaboration on utilities, cooperation in planning and development control, extended moratoriums on various interlocal actions, and a consolidation proposing the creation of a new type of general local government.[47] The new processes in Virginia have resulted in a substantial number of settlements, with several containing provisions unprecedented in the commonwealth and perhaps in the nation. On the basis of the number and diversity of these settlements, it may be contended that Virginia currently has one of the most dynamic environments in the country in terms of interlocal relations.

3

The Leesburg–Loudoun County Annexation Negotiations

This case study demonstrates the evolution of an intergovernmental negotiation. The parties to the case, a town and a county, are independent units of government in Virginia, and the negotiators were their elected and appointed public officials. The negotiations involved the parties for six months in dynamic, often adversarial and sometimes tension-filled situations. A formal negotiation process was used in which teams of negotiators and an independent mediator worked with the parties in both private sessions and joint meetings.

The parties entered the negotiation with polarized positions on the issues. Both local governments saw the dispute framed by state law as a win-lose contest with very important interests at stake. Each was committed to do what it could to clearly win in the negotiation, even though at the outset each felt that the talks were likely to be tentative and shortlived, with the courts finally resolving the dispute. Six months later, however, after twenty-five joint sessions and hundreds of hours in private meetings, the negotiating teams signed an agreement that not only encompassed the original disputed issues but also went much further, establishing new joint programs between the two local governments.

Key features of the successful negotiation have been identified through analysis of actual issues and party positions. These key features include: how the parties put proposals together, how they reacted to proposals, and how the seeds for settlement were developed from the issues and from the exchanges between the negotiators.

One significant finding revealed during the case documentation was that the analytic bargaining strategies used by each side were overwhelmed by the dynamics of the interactions between individuals as they expressed personal reactions to statements made by the other side along with their team role. These interpersonal negotiation dynamics went through four identifiable stages as the dispute evolved. Therefore, the case was organized into four evolutionary phases: (1) exploration and strategizing; (2) formal proposals; (3) confrontation; and (4) agreement seeking. These phases are discussed to point out how the major conditions of the negotiation changed as the talks progressed. As the parties' views of the issues changed, the parties altered the form of negotiation; thus, an internal structure for the negotiation evolved from the dynamics of the negotiation process. Some formal aspects of the structure were initially imposed by the mediator, then willingly accepted by the parties, and consisted of formal negotiating teams meeting in a joint session and caucus model. The two teams and the mediator thus formed a consciously organized environment for the negotiation, which was able to adapt to and support the various communication formats and inter-action styles encountered through the different phases of the process. In fact, through this negotiating structure the two teams and the mediator were able to maintain the negotiations process throughout certain highly adversarial periods that led to developing the settlement. How this structure evolved and how the parties' relationships developed over the course of the negotiation is described in the case study.

Following a short introduction describing the parties and the disputed issue, the case unfolds in sections corresponding to the four phases of the negotiation. The first section, Exploration and Strategizing, includes an extended description of the substantive issues that the reader may skip without losing the essence of the negotiation process. In the second section, Formal Proposals, the process of making proposals and counterproposals in the negotiation is described. Combined in the third section are descriptions of the third and fourth phases, Confrontation and Agreement Seeking, which overlapped in time. The final section, Review and Conclusions, begins with a summary of the main findings of the case, in terms of the external and internal support systems necessary for intergovernmental negotiation, then reviews the various roles the mediator performed in the case.

Introduction

Leesburg, the county seat of Loudoun County, Virginia, is a historic central market town of approximately 9,000 people in a productive agricultural setting.[1] The town and the county, which in 1982 totalled 57,000 people, have rapidly increased their population over the past decade, doubling in size because their location on the fringe of the Washington, D.C., metropolitan region has made them desirable to real estate developers, new businesses, and residents. This rapid growth and the corresponding demands for new public services have naturally led to expanded scope, capabilities, and resources of the two governments.

The annexation dispute between the town and county in 1982 was a contest between two growing governments over functional jurisdiction—that is, over which government ought to control land development policy in the area surrounding the town. Fundamentally, the dispute concerned the town's assertion of independence from the county and was complicated by the county's sense that a successful annexation by the town would set the stage for the town to become an independent city. The county negotiators' concern was based on their awareness of the serious implications for the county's tax base if the town did indeed become a city.

The underlying issues in the negotiation, the power relations between the town and county, reached beyond the initial issue brought by the town: a proposal to quadruple its size from about 3.5 square miles to more than 15 square miles by annexing surrounding county lands. The negotiators had to deal with both the underlying legal implications and the contrasting political values affecting the proposed annexation before they could come to terms on the annexation itself. The negotiating teams tackled these issues in several ways—through the exchange of formal proposals, through confrontation and distributive bargaining, and through problem solving and joint text-drafting techniques. After months of negotiation, the parties were finally able to drop their protective adversarial stances and fashion an agreement on the land to be annexed and the conditions of annexation that met each side's own internal requirements.

An interesting facet of this case is that when the parties reached agreement on annexation, what had been the major issue at the beginning of the case, settlement did not follow. Rather, a new issue surfaced that again positioned the parties as adversaries. The new issue concerned the ability of the localities to affect each other's viability as independent governments under existing laws. Ultimately the negotiators agreed to settlement terms that were contingent on the state legislature's enacting new legislation authorizing their agreement. After this legislation was adopted and both the state reviewing agency and the courts accepted the parties' agreements, the dispute was formally settled.

Mediation was introduced into this case because the parties had not been successful in previous direct negotiations over the same issue, and because the statute governing the state's annexation process specifically authorized and endorsed the mediation option in this class of interjurisdictional disputes. Moreover, the state agency with immediate jurisdiction in the case, the Virginia Commission on Local Government, actively encouraged the town and county to enter mediation. The parties were not hopeful that they could avoid extensive litigation and a court-ordered determination of the annexation; yet they agreed to enter negotiations with a mediator to try to settle the dispute without recourse to the court.

The Annexation Petition

Leesburg's formal filing of an annexation petition in the spring of 1982 came as something of a surprise to the county's leaders, who had been encouraging the town to resume a dialogue over the issue. The previous year the town had added some three hundred acres as a result of a landowner's petition to be annexed by the town. The county staff had objected to the transfer of that parcel to the town and had opposed the petition in court. Town-county relations, although functional, were strained. The town's initiative in constructing its own utility system, a larger system than the town itself needed, and its interest in annexation created for the county staff the specter of a town setting the stage to withdraw from the county entirely by becoming an independent city. Though the town denied this intent in its public "Resolution for Annexation," county officials were suspicious of the town leaders' real intent. The possibility of the town's transition to a city was the county's most fundamental concern. If it did so, the town would, under Virginia law, establish an independent tax base and thus withdraw a very considerable fiscal resource from the county. For the town, the issues centered on its right to determine the pattern of growth and development in areas surrounding the town without county interference. For both localities, the issues concerned the town's autonomy from the county in an important decisionmaking arena (land development) and the perception by each side that the other side wanted to exert local power to the detriment of town-county relations.

When in late 1981 the county discovered that the town was considering a formal petition to the state for annexation, the county staff began studying various legal options. In January and February 1982 the county attempted to initiate a negotiating process with the town under the auspices of the state's Commission on Local Government. The county's goal was to engage the town in negotiations to consider possible annexation for the town in exchange for permanent renunciation of its right to become a city. The town declined to participate in negotiations under this agenda. Instead, on March 10, 1982, the town council passed a formal resolution indicating its intent to annex. Later the council passed an annexation ordinance, and on April 6 it formally filed a petition for annexation with the state's Commission on Local Government.

Introduction of the Mediator

On April 22 town and county representatives met to begin a dialogue on the annexation issues. During the meeting the parties stated their positions on the issues and informally agreed to the appointment of a mediator for formal negotiations. On April 24 at a meeting in the state commission's offices, the parties formally agreed to try to negotiate settlement with the aid of an independent mediator. Also at this meeting, the parties first met the designated mediator and discussed certain organizational points, including the mediator's compensation (each locality agreed to pay half the mediation costs), a method for dealing with the media (the mediator would draft statements and releases), the composition of negotiating teams, and dates for initial negotiation sessions.

The mediator next met separately with the governing boards of the two localities to introduce his role and answer questions about how he intended to manage the negotiations process. He used the period to explore the issues with the governing boards and to try to understand the views each side held of the other side. He requested each locality to form a negotiating team that included two elected officials, the chief executive officer of the locality, and the attorneys in the case. The town had previously designated the town manager as their sole negotiator, but at the mediator's request they appointed the mayor and another councilman to the team. The town employed a special annexation counsel who did not join the negotiating team. The county board of supervisors appointed its chairman, another elected official, the county administrator, and the county attorney to the negotiating team. The county attorney and the town manager were designated as lead spokespersons for their respective sides, and they quickly developed as the chief strategists for most of the negotiation.

In initial private meetings with the mediator, each side was pessimistic over the chances for a negotiated settlement. The county negotiators were convinced that the town, particularly its manager and mayor, would be intractable in negotiations. They based this assumption on their experiences in the talks over the past year. The county staff felt that the town was going to try to get its annexation through the court process; the town manager felt that the county negotiators would not recognize the town's requirements for autonomy in managing its affairs and would inevitably refuse to agree to the town's annexation of a large tract of land. Both sides felt that the negotiations were likely to be perfunctory, impasses would quickly surface, and the negotiations would break down, leading directly to the courts. Each side's initial negotiating strategies were influenced less by expectations of extended, successful negotiations than by the desire to establish a record that they participated in good faith in negotiations while they lasted.

Phase 1: Exploration and Strategizing

The first negotiating session was on May 10, 1982, in the town council's conference room. At the mediator's request, earlier that week each side had prepared a list of issues it felt should be addressed in negotiations. The parties were instructed to bring to the negotiating table any issues they felt were important enough to affect the settlement, including issues beyond the confines of the immediate annexation proposal. The parties were not surprised about each other's lists, and the lists provided a framework from which a joint issue agenda was formed.

Each negotiator came to the negotiating table with different assumptions about the process. They were unsure of the dynamics of the formal negotiations and therefore wary of potential risks to their interests; they were uncertain of how to develop a strategy to best achieve their goals.

Initial Strategies

From the very first session, both the town and county negotiators made efforts to see and to portray the issues as tangible concerns to be won or lost either through negotiations or the courts. Both sides, in different ways, approached the negotiations as rational players intent on protecting the interests of their governments. Basic negotiating strategies were developed by the professional staff on each team—by the manager for the town and by the attorney and administrator for the county. As the negotiations developed, two individuals, the town manager and county attorney, began to lead strategy development for their teams. Both were committed to clearly defined *reasoned* negotiating strategies; both valued the ability to justify proposals in the context of the formal exposition of their team's interests or, when in joint session, in the interests of both teams. This reasoned-argument approach gave a degree of order to the negotiation, which allowed for fewer overt interventions by the mediator. The parties were largely self-regulating in maintaining the negotiating environment.

The elected officials on both teams played major roles in the negotiation but generally left the primary development of strategy to their professional staffs; the elected officials relied on their staffs' expertise and commitment to their respective government's interests. The staffs' negotiating strategies were shaped not only by the contrasting interests of their governments but significantly by the norms of their professions (government management or law). Thus, the negotiating strategies of the town manager and county administrator reflected the rational balancing of alternatives (settlement options versus the probabilities of a favorable court ordered settlement), and those of the county attorney reflected client interest advocacy.

The county team's initial strategy involved minimizing exposure of county positions (indeed, the county had not at this point internally committed itself to a consensus position on how much land it might negotiate away) while gathering as much information as possible about the town's intentions. This strategy was most strongly influenced by the county attorney, who saw the need to delay the state's annexation review process and to gather information on the annexation in order to build a better county case for either the negotiations or the expected litigation.

The application of the county's initial strategy had three major components. The first was to request a delay in the formal schedule set for review of the case. This delay, in the county's view, was needed to test the town's willingness to pursue negotiations seriously and it was a requirement for the county's continued participation in negotiations. The second component was to get the town to provide information to the county—data useful for either negotiation or litigation. The final component of the county's strategy was to place the county's issues on the negotiating table instead of the town's sole issue of the annexation. The most important county issue concerned the possibility of the town's becoming an independent city. The county sought to move the negotiations toward this issue by proposing to grant an annexation only if the town would give up its right to become a city.

The town approached negotiations confident about the review of its annexation case by the state commission and with a consensus from the town council in favor of the annexation. Since the beginning of the annexation proceedings, the town manager had a clear view of a compromise to settle the dispute, which he conveyed to the mediator, but he was not optimistic about the possibilities for negotiating that settlement.

The town's initial strategy for the negotiations was to demonstrate to the public, to the state agency, and ultimately to the court the town's good faith in attempting to find a peaceful settlement to the dispute. In developing the annexation petition, the town manager had laid out a case that he felt was fully defensible in court, given support from expert counsel. He felt the town had a strong case for annexation, and that the county's resistance was to be expected (he had prepared the town council for a period of unpleasantness in town-county relations). He had predicated the annexation action on the statutory means for adding land to his community: a trial before a specially convened, three-judge panel drawn from around the state. In short, the manager's strategy for the negotiations was based on having a viable alternative to negotiations.

Given that premise, the town took a wait-and-see attitude in the negotiations while looking for signs on the county's part of conciliation and a willingness to give the town what it needed—a bottom-line compromise annexation. The town was prepared to make concessions from its original annexation petition when it judged the time was right. Its immediate action was to go along with the county's requested delay in the petition before the state commission and if the county demonstrated that it would indeed grant land to the town, to put the town's compromise offer on the table. In effect, while agreeing to participate in the negotiations, the town's primary strategy was to rely on the basic annexation process as the means of achieving its ends. This strategy made the town a rather cautious negotiator, willing to go along with the game for the present, but very much taking a wait-and-see attitude before reaching out to settlement.

The Issues

The first three negotiating sessions, each held roughly a week apart, gave the parties their first experience in formal team negotiations with a mediator. The parties began by sizing up one another, looking to see where the other team stood on the issues. In the first session, on May 10, the parties presented the topics they wanted to bring to the negotiating table. They also discussed the need for a joint agreement to postpone programmed actions by the state commission that would put time pressure on the negotiators. They discussed their sense of the meaning of the phrase "good faith negotiations," and the elected officials on each team made statements that, in effect, were calls for reason and restraint on both sides. Each side was tentatively committed to negotiations at the outset, and each was most wary of the possibility of giving away more than might be gained from the process. Each team was comfortable with its own makeup, feeling a real sense of internal control and management. Neither side felt it had a "loose cannon," an uncontrollable individual on the team. Throughout most of the negotiation, team solidarity was apparent on both sides.

At the mediator's request, the parties had separately identified subjects for negotiation; each party identified three or four major issues and approximately ten subsidiary issues. In the meeting a list of common issues was prepared, with the mediator acting as a recorder for the negotiators.

The Town Annexation Issue. The first and major issue in the dispute was what land the town should annex. At the first session, however, the county attempted to redefine this land issue by raising the following questions: Why does the town need to annex any land? Can't the county meet the town's needs in another way? And, if the town does need some new land, why does it need the very large land area it petitioned for? Given the major costs involved, how does the town justify the proposed annexation to its own citizens, to the county citizens, and to both governments? The county's spokesman, the county attorney, through a prepared line of questioning, was trying to move the county from a defensive stance opposing the annexation petition to a more active position in the negotiation. The town's legal options were not questioned; but in broadly refocusing the issues, the county was injecting its own view of the situation—that annexation was unnecessary and actually burdensome to both county and town residents.

The town negotiators had a mixed reaction to the county's initiative. The mayor reacted strongly to the negative presumptions he saw throughout the county's presentation. He felt the county's attitude toward the town was condescending. It was this very attitude, he stressed, that had led to the annexation petition. The town manager refused to challenge the county on the issues it raised and instead stated that he was present to negotiate on the annexation petition (that is, on the land issue) and he hoped that the county would request a formal explanation of the annexation. He offered to make a presentation at the next meeting on the details of the town's annexation petition.

The City Status Issue. The second issue for negotiation involved the town's possible attempt to become a city. This issue was raised by the county team and figured prominently as a major subnegotiation both early and late in the negotiations. The possibility that the town might become a city was critically important to the county because, under Virginia statutes, a city is a completely independent unit of government, fully separate from its surrounding county; it has its own school system, independent services, and, most importantly, its own tax base. Virginia towns, however, are a more limited form of local government: they are structurally part of counties, their schools are county schools, and their courts are county courts. Because towns are part of their surrounding county, the real property and other taxes in the towns are also part of the county's tax base.

Leesburg, the county seat and largest town in Loudoun County, provides a significant proportion of the county's nonrural tax base. The town's transition to a city would create major problems for the county government because it would lose the town's contribution to its tax base. The possibility that Leesburg would become a city so concerned the county team that it made clear that unless some accommodation was reached on this issue, the county would fight any annexation in court (negotiation would be impossible). In the county's view, annexation without some restraint on the town's ability to become a city would give the town a better case for transition to city status at some future date.

In a sense the city transition issue was given life by the presence of active negotiations. It would not have been such an issue before a court convened to judge the annexation petition because it dealt with prospective behavior by a future governing board, not a current factual action before the court for adjudication. Yet after the first few meetings, as the town negotiators listened to the county's message and the mediator privately confirmed the necessity of addressing this issue, the town negotiators acknowledged that the issue must be addressed if a negotiated settlement was to be reached.

The county perceived that the very scale of the town's annexation petition possibly could be intended to create viable boundaries for a new city. At the very first meeting, the county asked the town formally to follow a statutory provision whereby a town permanently renounces its right to become a city in exchange for the right to annex county land by ordinance—that is, without county opposition. The town negotiators rejected this proposal out of hand and made evident that they would not renounce permanently a statutory right that they possessed and that some future town council might find desirable. According to the town negotiators, the town council had no desire to become a city council, and the issue did not really belong in the negotiation. However, recognizing that the county was insistent upon addressing the issue of future city status, the town's negotiators agreed that it be made part of the negotiations.

At the second negotiating session, the county again tried to interest the town in renouncing its right to become a city. The county team indicated that, should the town voluntarily renounce city status as provided under the law, the county would be prepared to negotiate a reasonable settlement of the annexation dispute. The county was encouraged in its proposal by both a recent town-county annexation dispute that had been resolved in this way and by Leesburg's extremely well-defined image as a medium-sized historic town. The county negotiators were hoping that the town's elected officials would respond to the proposal to give the town more land and to identify its future with a town form of government—a smaller, more intimate government than offered in most cities.

The county negotiators were forthright about their concerns. One of the team's elected officials said that renunciation was the biggest issue to the county, and that even the possibility of the town's becoming a city put a chill on town-county cooperation, particularly in locating new commercial and industrial development around the town. He explained that the prevailing county policy of locating new development around existing communities would be foolish if those communities became cities and took away the very tax base the county had established there—the county, by following such progressive land planning practices, might well be digging its own fiscal grave. The implied alternative, not lost on the town negotiators, was that if these negotiations were unsuccessful, the county would begin to steer growth away from the Leesburg area and would not invest as heavily in new public infrastructure within the town's boundaries since town conversion to city status was at some point likely. The land use and economic interests of the communities were driving the negotiations.

The town manager responded to the county's presentation with the point that the town was not now seeking to become a city, but it wasn't about to give up the right to do so. In a public information pamphlet published prior to the negotiations, the town had discussed the possibility of renouncing its right ever to become a city. The town manager repeated some of this discussion including that the "possibility of city conversion is a strong negotiating tool which should be retained in Leesburg's future dealings with Loudoun County." This point generated a strong response: county negotiators quickly brought into question the good faith of the town in negotiations, then the parties jumped to confrontations across the negotiating table.

In the second meeting the town manager proposed "as a framework for the negotiations process, that we put city status behind us" by accepting a town proposal that the town would agree not to become a city within ten years following a negotiated annexation. The county negotiators responded that ten years' protection wasn't sufficient, and one of the county's elected officials stated that ten, twenty, or fifty years wouldn't make a difference. The county then proposed that it make a presentation the next week on the benefits for both sides of "permanent renunciation," even though the town had clearly stated its unwillingness to follow that approach. Not unexpectedly, the town totally rejected the county's presentation at the following meeting. The impasse was not fatal because the county was prepared for this rejection and because both sides wanted to move on and see proposals on the land issue of, on the one hand, how much land the county would be willing to give the town in a negotiated annexation and, on the other, how much the town would fall back from its original petition.

After these first three meetings the parties had developed a familiarity with each other and with the new negotiating environment. Though they were at impasse over the issue of city status, they felt it premature to break off negotiations at this point and agreed to concentrate on the land issue for the present. The city status issue, broadened to include the possibility that even the county might become a city, returned as a major dispute later in the negotiations, after the land issues were successfully negotiated. At the early stage in negotiations, the city status issue served to uncover for each party the particular sensitivities that the other team carried into the negotiations. It was not until much later in the negotiations, however, that both teams were to understand, internalize, and use these perceptions to modify their substantive positions. The first confrontations provided experience in practicing interteam exchange, in attempting to rationalize positions from one side to the other, and in dealing with the rejection that accompanies such calculated positioning in negotiations.

The Land Use Management Issues. The third issue on the agenda for negotiations was land use planning to manage growth development in the area around the town. The subject was first raised by the county negotiators. Over the past years, the county's governing board and staff had supported a strong environmental conservation ethic in their decisionmaking. The county was known to take active positions in favor of closely managing the land use conversion process in the county, controlling densities in new developments, and bargaining with developers to extract such concessions as school sites, construction of public facilities, and community investments before approving zoning changes and subdivision plans. Strong land use planning backed by tough zoning and subdivision management had become a point of pride in Loudoun County government. During 1981 the county had invested significant staff time (staff costs amounted to over $100,000) in a Leesburg Area Management Plan (LAMP).[2] The plan was developed by the county planning staff for the county planning commission and county supervisors. The town manager, in particular, saw the LAMP as an obstacle to the town's control of the land conversion process on its borders. He cited these two basic reasons for the annexation filing: constraints in the LAMP process and that the county, not the town, controlled land management around the town.

Early in 1981 and again in 1982 as the annexation petition was being prepared, the county had asked Leesburg to participate in the LAMP approval process by appointing citizens to a joint town-county committee to manage the development of the LAMP's policies. The town did so, but at the same time it was engaged in developing its own plan for the town and surrounding area. In the town's view, the LAMP was a county document to which the town might only give advisory opinions, which was much less satisfactory than a planning process under the town's exclusive control. The most significant differences between the town's plan and the LAMP were in the density limits (residential and commercial). The county wanted significantly lower residential densities in the developing areas around Leesburg than did the town.

Other Issues. The last issue the parties put on the negotiating table during the first meeting was summarized as "sharing resources and liabilities." At the opening of the meeting, when the discussion was nonadversarial and the parties were not emphasizing their positions on the touchy issues, the negotiators identified a few areas where greater cooperation could enable town and county governments to be more effective, save money, or deliver better salaries. The parties discussed the utility of using a common system to bill taxes for both governments, and of having the county contribute to the town's expenses for a public prosecutor, a town jail, and a regional police training academy. They talked about possible joint county and town efforts in extending the town's cable TV service in the county and mentioned maintaining a special farmland preservation tax program on any annexed farmland. These subissues, though interesting, were not controlling issues in the negotiation.

Town Perceptions About the Negotiations

During the early phases of the negotiations, the town's negotiators were suspicious of the county's willingness to accept them as equals in the tasks of government. This view was based not only on the current negotiations but on their interpretation of town-county relations over the years. The mayor, a lifelong town resident, made clear his strongly held feelings on this subject during the negotiating sessions. He made the assertion that although the town did not want to become a city, it would not let the county push it around as in the past and stated that the town is "a sophisticated and credible local government, capable of managing its town affairs and the new land in the annexation." The town manager made the same point, though in a cooler tone. He noted that the town managed government affairs, including planning and development policy, quite as well as the county and that "whatever the historic difference in their relative capabilities for public management, today, clearly, the town is not inferior to the county in its ability to provide efficient public services to its residents."

Throughout the beginning of the negotiation, the town negotiators expressed their feeling that the county treated the town in a paternalistic manner, as a subordinate level of government.

The town felt that negotiations would be perfunctory precisely because the county negotiators would not accede to what the town saw as its legitimate interests in managing the land surrounding the town by the direct method of annexing it and making it subject to town zoning powers. By providing utilities services in the developing areas and holding on to its options with respect to city status in the future, the town was committing itself to an independent course. The reality and the perception of control over land development policy and over the town government function were major underlying themes in the negotiation.

The town staff and, in particular, the town manager assumed a rather pained stance toward the county's demands for negotiations based on detailed factual data. In the manager's view, negotiations involved the establishment of positions, then the attempt to exchange proposals and reach a compromise. He was willing to follow the county's lead of looking for an information base for a reasonable length of time because he felt the county team was unable to come to grips with the central issue of giving up county land to the town. His demands for comparable information from the county staff were made basically to impose on the county staff the same time demands that answering the county's questions imposed on him.

The mediator called a meeting of professional staffs between the second and third negotiating sessions to specify the information that each side was requesting from the other. At the meeting the county delivered a ten-page list of questions, to which the town manager reacted by asking if the questions were meant for the negotiations or as interrogatories to be used in court. The town believed the county staff was intent on cornering it to demonstrate the weakness of the town's case for annexation. Unsurprisingly, not only did the town reject the premise but it refused to play the data game by the county's rules.

County Perceptions About the Negotiations

The county team was not only disappointed by the town's unwillingness in the previous negotiating session to modify its proposed annexation but it was losing interest in the negotiations because it believed the town's active defense of its annexation petition indicated inflexibility on the key boundary location issue. After two sessions the county was blocked on its initiative to get the town to renounce its right to city status. Nevertheless, the county team decided that it still had potentially more to gain than lose by remaining in the negotiations.

At least three considerations influenced the county's decision to remain in negotiations. First, the county team, even before the onset of negotiations, thought their main chance to negotiate a settlement lay with recently elected members of the town council who had not yet taken office. Thus, the county was encouraged to remain in negotiations at least until the new team had taken its place in town government.

Second, the county's overall strategy for dealing with the annexation issue, shaped in large part by the county attorney, involved gathering as much information as possible about the town's managerial capacity to handle the annexation. Although the county felt that it needed this information to negotiate a settlement, it had another reason for obtaining it: information gathered through the negotiations process could be invaluable should the negotiations break down and court maneuvering lie ahead. As long as the town delivered hard data on the town's fiscal situation and other issues, the county team had a practical rationale for remaining in negotiations.

A third reason the county remained in negotiations is that the mediator strongly indicated to the county negotiators that the town was flexible on the crucial issue of the boundary line. The first two reasons for remaining in negotiations were undoubtedly the controlling ones because they were derived exclusively from the negotiators' own analyses. Yet the mediator's intervention, an external view supporting a decision to remain in negotiations, was also compelling.

The county negotiators insisted they would proceed only if they could work from reliable data about the proposed area to be annexed and the town's fiscal ability to manage it. The county staff members particularly emphasized the need for specific answers to questions about the town, its finances, its commitments to provide public services, and other items. They expressed an intent to undertake a technical analysis of the town's needs and grant annexation concessions only if the hard data provided by the town offered analytic and rational justifications for doing so. This approach served the county team's immediate purpose of gaining as much town information as possible. Of course, it angered the town negotiators, who saw it as a stalling strategy; some team members felt it was another example of the county's attempt to dictate town actions that were against the town's interests.

Although these interactions created tensions on both sides, the mediator felt it unnecessary to intervene in the substance of the dialogue. He considered working with each party to reshape their inquiries and responses, but decided (appropriately, in retrospect) that the parties didn't need to solve the data issue—they needed to allow their attitudes to surface and to expose their strategies. The data conflict was the vehicle for this expression, and neither party was willing to give up the negotiation over the data issue. Sensing this, the mediator limited his interventions in the exchanges to facilitation sorties—that is, he occasionally interrupted heated dialogue and asked the parties to restate positions and to listen clearly to statements made—with the objective of proceeding the talks and defusing tense situations. On occasion he called for caucus sessions so the parties could go over the preceding dialogue with only their own team present. The mediator rejected the opportunity to intervene on the substantive issues of the data dispute because he judged that to do so would be to legitimize the issue and make it more of a cause for real dispute than for maneuvering. He also wanted to restrict his substantive interventions so they would be fresh when needed in critical situations.

Phase 2: Formal Proposals

The second phase in the negotiation began with the county's first proposal to address the proposed annexation, and ended with the settlement of that issue: a negotiated new boundary line that more than tripled the town's size. In this phase, which lasted over two months, the parties held five joint negotiating sessions and numerous separate meetings with the mediator. During this phase the negotiators formed positions on a range of issues, cast these into formal written proposals, and presented the proposals in joint sessions. Upon receiving a proposal, negotiators usually caucused to talk privately and formulate response positions, as well as to design counterproposals for subsequent meetings. Through this formal process, designed and managed by the mediator, the parties narrowed the issues significantly. They used the process to trade concessions, slowly uncovering their more closely held positions. They also introduced new ideas derived in part from listening to proposals made by the other side. Through a reciprocal process of stating their own requirements on focused issues, the parties finally created a jointly held understanding of the situation that supported the fashioning of agreements on issues previously locked in impasses.

For the most part, the negotiations in this phase were competitive: They were marked by strategizing for advantage and self-protection, by very evident conflict among individuals over underlying issues regarding the extent of county influence over town decisionmaking, and by the feeling among the county negotiators that the town's leadership was moving the town away from traditional and positive town-county relations. Yet these conflicts and competitive strategy formulation did not so occupy the parties that they were unable to focus on the substantive issues in dispute. The process of making formal proposals and counterproposals carried each side's arguments across the table. Eventually, through repeated exposure to their opponent's package of positions, each party began to recognize that the other side's demands might be accommodated with its own requirements in a comprehensive settlement.

The description of the second phase outlines how settlement of the land issues evolved.

The County's First Proposal

At the beginning of the formal proposal phase the parties were very far apart on what they viewed as acceptable settlement terms on the basic issue of how much land the town should get. The town's petition for annexation, which was reaffirmed during initial negotiations in early May, was for approximately 9,500 acres, or over 15 square miles. The county's first proposal offered the town 420 acres, about 5 percent of the town's request. Only 90 acres were vacant land ready for future expansion of the town; 330 acres were developed, mostly as subdivisions on the edge of town.

The county's proposal was formally presented in a written document. In introducing the proposal, county team members took turns offering individualistic views of the proposal's merits, in a preorchestrated presentation. For example, one member acted conciliatory, one tough, and so forth. This lengthy process was intended to assure the town negotiators that the county had rationally analyzed the situation and was making a good-faith offer based on the facts of the town's real needs. The effect, however, was to communicate to the town negotiators the county's negative feeling that the town's petition for annexation was unreasonable, far in excess of the town's requirements. The county negotiators were, in fact, using the formal proposal to deny the town's annexation initiative. The town understood the county proposal to be a rejection of the town's need for an annexation. This approach angered members of the town negotiating team.

As part of the presentation, the county's planner revealed a technical study with maps showing that the projected growth rates for the Leesburg area suggested that only several hundred acres would be converted from farmland to urban uses in the next decade; the thousands of acres the town was seeking would remain agricultural and rural land for the foreseeable future. The county attorney made the point that the county's offer of 420 acres was intended to meet the town's needs for the next ten years—the minimum period allowed between annexation petitions. Thus the county's guiding annexation principle was much different than the town's. The town wanted to get enough land to allow it to determine the pace, timing, and location of land development and public improvements in its own geographic area—that is, to move away from what the town perceived as the county's primary role in land use management in the area surrounding the town.

The county addressed other issues in its proposal. The most important issue was a thirty-year moratorium on the town's conversion to a city.

By proposing a moratorium, the county acknowledged for the first time the town's firm position rejecting any offer that required them to renounce permanently their right to become a city. The county took this step with considerable reluctance and regarded it as a main concession. Because annexation was permanent and nonrevocable, the county had wanted very much to dispose permanently of the city status issue. Yet in private meetings with the mediator the county staff noted that their interests could be adequately protected if, as a result of the negotiations, the county could get a binding agreement whereby the town could not become a city for an extended time period. In dealing with this issue, and in forging negotiating positions on the annexation boundary, the problem of generating a consensus within a negotiating team led to internal negotiations and deliberations that sometimes were as extended as the interteam exchanges. In these discussions the teams' lead negotiators—the county attorney and the town manager—became advocates of positions and strategies, taking the lead in forming alternatives for consideration by the rest of the team members.

The county's proposal to give the town 420 acres in exchange for a thirty-year moratorium on city status was poorly received by the town. In a caucus after hearing the county's explanation of its proposal, the town negotiators characterized the county offer as laughable, as a joke. At this point the negotiations seemed very tenuous, and the process was on the edge of breaking down. In the view of several town negotiators, the county's proposal was ample evidence that the county was not willing either to deal with the town as an equal or to accept the town's need to shape its own growth, with the consequent requirement for a sizable annexation; the county offer appeared as another example of county attempts to preserve the town as a client government, dependent upon the county for major decisions.

The town manager saw the situation differently. In his view, the fact that the county had actually addressed the land issue, however meagerly from the town perspective, gave the town team the negotiating room they needed to put a counterproposal on the table. The parties had agreed at the last joint session to set aside two consecutive nights for continuation of the negotiations. The county offered its proposal the first night, and the town had agreed to respond the second night.

The Town's Counterproposal

Having received a proposal from the county that addressed the crucial land issue, the town negotiators proceeded to put forward their first real effort to settle the dispute. Up to this point, the town had listened to the county's initiatives, had agreed to a delay on state action on their petition, and had received a county proposal, however unacceptable, that for the first time addressed the critical land issue directly. Days earlier, before the county had put forward its proposal, town negotiators had worked out their counterproposal, which at the time they understood as their first and perhaps last effort to reach an accord.

The town's ultimate goal for the negotiations, indeed probably for the entire court-oriented annexation process, was to wind up with an annexation line that largely followed a proposed boundary created by the county's planning staff called the Leesburg Area Urban Limit Line. This urban limit line (ULL)—the line around the town within which future development should be contained and not allowed to spill over— extended roughly three miles from the town in all directions and included almost half of the land area that the town had formally petitioned for. The town's proposal exceeded the ULL and totalled approximately 6,000 acres. The ULL seemed an obvious compromise between the very large area originally sought by the town and the limited area the county seemed prepared to give the town. The ULL had, after all, been created by the county's own staff as a logical limit to urban expansion. To the county negotiators, however, the ULL was a limit for the distant future, a guide for long range planning policy, not a vehicle for deciding current issues of size and scale of municipal government.

In effect the town was putting its major concession, its offer for settlement of the annexation line, on the table. In the town's view this line was likely the same line they would get from a court-ordered annexation. Thus, their counterproposal modified their original proposal as much as they felt appropriate. The town negotiators had not, to this point, invested their hopes in a negotiated settlement. In the negotiations leading to this counterproposal, the town had remained unconvinced that the county would accept any negotiated settlement that gave the town most of what it was seeking; the county's first proposal (420 acres) confirmed this belief. Yet the town felt it appropriate to put forward its major offer. If the county was willing to continue to negotiate on the basis of this offer, the town would get its land through a negotiated settlement. If the county rejected the offer out of hand (the town privately thought this likely), then negotiations would be over and the town could clearly feel and state that they had given the negotiations option a clear chance. (These positions were held privately by the town, they were not communicated as threats.)

The town proposal, a fifteen-page document, started with a review of the county's proposal of the previous evening and a rebuttal of certain points. The formal counterproposal covered twelve points, beginning with a boundary line that generally followed the ULL except for an expansion of the line to bring the Leesburg Airport within the town.

TABLE 3.1
Negotiations After the First Round of Proposals

Major Issues	Town Counterproposal	County Proposal
Land to be annexed	6000 acres	420 acres
Moratorium on town conversion to city status to follow annexation	N	30 years
Moratorium on town and on county conversion to city status to follow annexation	10 years	N

N = no offer

The town repeated in its counterproposal an offer made in the first phase of negotiations: the town would not become a city for a period of ten years following the negotiated settlement.

Negotiation Status

At this point in negotiations the county and the town had each presented a major written proposal. Two basic issues stood out and were addressed in each: (1) the amount and location of land area to be annexed by the town and (2) differences over the number of years before the town could seek to become a city. Except for addressing subsidiary issues for which there were no great disagreements, it looked at though compromises on these two issues would lead directly to a written agreement. The parties appeared to have consciously reshaped their positions into a common sense of the nature of the issues. The major issues and positions of the county's first proposal and the town's counterproposal could be put into a single table (see Table 3.1), suggesting that simple compromise might carry the day. It looked like the parties were talking the same language, even though they were for the moment still far apart on the numbers.

In fact, the parties had not reached understandings on the currency for bargaining. Each side, the county in particular, was using the language of joint concerns (units of land and years) as a vehicle representing ideas that were primarily construed in defensive and self-protective contexts. Each side attributed meanings to their proposal other than those they actually communicated across the negotiating table. It was, in reality, too early to attempt to settle the dispute. Each side had a defensive strategy based on the assumption that the other side could not be trusted to make the compromises necessary to settle the dispute. Moreover, each side had yet to mature as a negotiating team. As negotiations brought forth new positions and the individual team members reacted, the teams experienced their own internal dynamics of team leadership and ways of dealing with controversies.

Both teams, during most of the negotiations, were led by full-time staff in joint sessions and in development of positions. The county side had greater staff resources—the county administrator coordinated the team, the county attorney organized the strategy and was often the designated spokesperson, and the planner's office undertook a major part in analyzing proposals. The town depended greatly on the town manager, who organized the negotiating strategy after coordination with elected officials, supervised analysis of positions, and was the chief spokesperson for the town. Staff played a continuing and dominant role throughout the negotiations; however, at different points along the way elected officials on each side stepped in and redirected the course of the negotiations.

The tensions of the negotiation process often placed the team that was receiving a proposal in a stressful situation. In a typical exchange the lead negotiator on the side making the proposal would describe the reasoning behind the proposal as a way of explaining it to the other side. Explanations of the initial proposals typically were met with stony looks as the receiving team asked one or two perfunctory questions and then requested a caucus. At different times in caucus members of each team, both elected officials and administrative staff, suggested withdrawing from the negotiations because the other side wasn't "serious" and therefore couldn't be trusted. Almost always, however, one or more individuals within a team could look past the frustration of the issue of the moment and thus hold the pieces together.

The mediator intervened in these caucus sessions as the advocate for maintaining the negotiations process. To counter the intense frustration felt by the negotiators, he would review presentations to keep the team focused on the substance of the proposal and not on their negative characterizations of it. On occasion he would assure teams that in discussions with the other side he had become convinced that there was more negotiating room on the issues—that counterproposals would be reciprocated and that new positions would be drawn out that were now being held back. At the early stages in the process of swapping formal proposals, the mediator encouraged the development of full, formal written proposals addressing eight or ten issues. He early rejected as inappropriate the model of separating the parties and carrying messages back and forth.

In the process of forming proposals, the staff formally solicited direction from elected officials, then laid out alternatives with the staff's preferred directions indicated. Generally, the elected officials on each side deferred to staff recommendations about strategy; but on occasion in crucial situations, elected officials made clear their preferences and staff quickly deferred.

The Seed of Settlement

In addition to adjusting the requested amount of land needed for annexation and calling for a ten-year moratorium on the town's possible conversion to city status, the town's proposal included an offer that later proved to be the basis for a major part of the settlement. The most significant theme underlying the annexation dispute was whether the town or the county should control the land development process around the town. Though a primary goal of the town was to annex certain major developed subdivisions, the town also was mindful of the desirability of shaping land use patterns in newly developing areas according to its preferences. If the land was not annexed, the county would set zoning policy and would determine the placement of public facilities to support development. The town negotiators saw the county's concerns with growth management around Leesburg as a constant example of the county's decisions based on its own best interest rather than on Leesburg's best interest. The issue was made sharper for the town when the technical requirements for the new wastewater treatment plant it was building indicated that the town would be better off financially if it could develop area surrounding the town limits so that area could share the service provision costs with the existing service population.

Despite these considerations that argued for the town's exclusive control over land development as a prime rationale for annexation, the town's counterproposal included the following initiative:

> Land use and development phasing: The town and county will plan and phase growth in line with a joint county-town plan arrived at in separate negotiations for the annexation area. The county planning agencies will act as planning agencies in the annexation for the term of the agreement. Leesburg and Loudoun will prohibit urban growth beyond the new boundary except by agreement of both.[3]

This proposal went to the heart of the county's objection to the town's annexation of thousands of vacant acres: once the town exclusively managed the land, it could rezone agricultural land so that speculators and developers might be encouraged to engage in what the county viewed as overly rapid development. The county feared that once it lost control of the land development process, it would be required to provide new schools, roads, and other expensive infrastructure to support the too rapid development.

The town's proposal was built upon the county's land management plan (LAMP), yet effectively reversed the basic power relationships underlying it. The town's proposal was to share land-use policymaking with the county. The town even suggested that the county's planning agencies be designated to implement the policy, giving further credence to the joint nature of the undertaking. It was immediately apparent to the county, however, that the land would be town land and that the county would be a contributor to town policy, which would reverse the current situation in which the town was invited to participate in making county land policy.

The county recognized that the town's new offer to move the annexation lines to the ULL and to include the county in the formulation of town land use policy, was a significant change in position. The county team caucused for over an hour to review the town's proposal. After the caucus, the county expressed disappointment that the line did not follow the ULL exactly and in certain places substantially exceeded it. The county attorney indicated that his team needed to study the proposal and gather specific information from the town about the proposal before responding. He suggested that the town's apparent policy that all growth in the area had to be within town boundaries didn't fit county policy and wasn't necessary; he supported this assertion by citing examples from other communities in the area. The chairman of the county supervisors, who was the senior official on the county team, said he thought the town had made a serious proposal that he would not now reject. He said that "in fact, it could form a future basis for agreement."

The county then suggested that the next negotiating session be spent reviewing both the county's proposal and the town's counterproposal in more depth. In a sharp response the town manager said that he hoped the county would do more than pose questions at the next meeting because each side should get down to serious negotiations; the questions should be posed and asked at the staff level between negotiating sessions. The county expressed concern at what they viewed as an effort to speed up negotiations and to specify too closely the agenda for the next joint meeting. The county did not want to be on record as agreeing to come up with a new proposal just yet.

The County's Counterproposal

The next negotiating session a week later was mainly a county-dominated session, reviewing the implications of the town's previous proposal. The dialogue began with the county's asking the town manager to explain why the boundaries in the town proposal exceeded the ULL by about 1,200 acres. The county team then described its view of the ULL concept, one that differed substantially from the town's understanding. The county spokesperson summarily rejected the town's proposed ten-year moratorium on city transition as being insufficient for both the town and county. His presentation moved next to the land planning issue and he suggested that the proper vehicle for a joint plan would be the county's new but not yet completed Leesburg Area Plan, the new LAMP. The town manager disagreed, interjecting his view that a new planning process was indeed needed—one adopted by both governing boards, one with a more balanced source of authority.

The parties reviewed numerous other issues, finding agreement on some, but reasons for adversarial positions on most. At one point the town manager complained that the county had not responded to the town's requests for information on issues, even though the county had made its demands for information from the town a basic test of good faith in negotiations. A member of the county team was stung and reacted sharply, creating an unplanned and tense moment between the parties. During the long caucus that followed, members of the county team, frustrated at being forced away from their preferred solution, discussed quitting the negotiations. Finally, however, the county decided to remain in the negotiations and to submit a new proposal they had developed that the county attorney had been refining over the past several weeks. In the meantime, they would formally respond to the town's questions.

The county's new proposal attempted to maintain the county's primary control over the zoning and conversion of farmland in the area surrounding the town. The county called the proposal a phased annexation. In effect the county was offering to the town a relatively large land area in stages over a ten-year time period. The map the county presented had three colors that represented three phases; each phase addressed specific time periods and development criteria under which the county would transfer specific major land parcels to the town. Under the proposal the town would immediately get only a relatively small amount of land that was fully developed. As additional vacant land became ready to be developed according to negotiated criteria, it too could be annexed by the town.

The total land offered by the county was considerably greater in this proposal than in the first one; yet it was much less than the land encompassed by the town's counterproposal. Nevertheless, the county's offer indicated that the county would agree to cede large areas of county land to the town if its interests in managing the land conversion process were met. Also promising was that the boundary for the third phase of annexation would be the same as the boundary of the town's utility service area; obtaining this larger area was a major goal for the town. The county proposal repeated the demand from its first proposal for the town's thirty-year renunciation of its right to city status. The proposal also addressed a number of other issues with offers attractive to the town, the county, or both parties.

As had become the practice, the town negotiators called for a caucus after listening to the county presentation of its proposal. The town had not anticipated the phased annexation proposal and did not want to reject it out of hand. Town negotiators initially reacted by indicating that although the areas assigned in each phase were much too limited, the phasing approach might be acceptable if those areas were substantially enlarged.

On returning to the negotiating table, the town manager gave the county rather positive feedback about the proposal. However, when the mediator suggested that the proposal become the basis for a town response, the manager reminded the mediator that both the last town proposal and the current county proposal were still on the table. Despite this caution, the town's generally positive response left the county team feeling they had carried the day and that their concept of phased annexation ultimately would be accepted by the town.

The Town's Response and the Mediator's Intervention

During the next week the town's negotiators took a closer look at the phased annexation proposal and rejected it. The concept, they felt, was cumbersome and would not give the town as much control over its destiny as would either the straightforward single-stage annexation in their proposal or the traditional court annexation process. The county, on the other hand, in staff meetings since the previous session had become more and more convinced that the phased annexation concept was workable, was in the county's interest, and ultimately could be sold to the town. Moreover, the county staff felt that the negotiating process kept eroding their bottom lines; they felt they were always in a position of being asked to give up more and more of the county. Some staff members believed strongly that the county had compromised too much already and that it shouldn't let itself be pushed around by the town. In their opinion the town ought to see the sense in the county's phased annexation offer, and if it didn't, the issue should go to court. There was a real sentiment on the county team to break the cycle of compromise—to either accept the last county proposal or go to court.

The mediator picked up these sentiments in meetings with the county team over the next few days. And from town negotiators he had learned that the town was leaning away from the phased annexation approach. In fact the town had decided to reject the phased annexation concept and pursue a modified version of its own approach. The mediator perceived a widening gap and hardening of positions between the parties that the parties could not perceive (there had been no ex parte contacts since the previous negotiating session); therefore, he stated this concern to both sides without conveying each side's rejection of the other's proposal since these positions might yet change. He also requested the staff from the two teams to meet prior to the next scheduled negotiating session. The county's staff resisted this meeting because they were anticipating how pressure would be imposed. The mediator, feeling that the town's decision to reject the county's phased approach must not be dropped on the table at a formal session, pushed for the staff-level meeting. Prior to that meeting he reviewed the county's interests with the town manager, reinforcing the idea that any proposal the county might accept must substantively address the issue of the county's role in land use management.

At the staff meeting the town manager did not explicitly reject the phased annexation approach, but he suggested that the town wanted to return to its last proposal modified with new roles for the county in land use management. The county staff, as they listened to these points, understood that the town probably was not going to accept the phased annexation approach on which they were counting so heavily. The county staff had a few days before the scheduled negotiating session to analyze the situation with the county's elected officials and to develop their position further. A lively debate ensued within the county over its further participation in negotiations. In the end the county's negotiators came to the next joint meeting prepared to hear the town reject the phased annexation and if the town proposal was rich enough, to renegotiate on it.

A Framework for Settlement

For three consecutive evenings beginning on July 27, the negotiating teams exchanged proposals on the land area, the issue of possible city status for the town, a shared land development policy, and roughly ten other issues of secondary importance that, if not settled, might have given rise to a spiraling impasse and breakdown. The parties were not yet committed to settling the dispute, and they might still have decided to break off negotiations if some impasse developed.

On the first night of the new series of intensive negotiations, the county team reintroduced the phased annexation concept as its framework for settling the dispute. As expected, the town manager indicated that there were major policy differences over this concept and that perhaps they could use another mechanism to reach the county's goals. One of the county team members, an elected official, expressed irritation and asked the manager to be specific. The county team thought it had sold the phased annexation concept to the town team at the last meeting. Now, it was discovering that the town was rejecting its proposal, and it resented the fact enormously.

The town's new concept was based on its previous proposal for a single major annexation, but with certain new interlocal agreements that would bind the town to a set of formal policies governing county interests in land development in the annexed area. These policies would give the county a clear role in determining land use policy in the annexed territory. The town's new proposal also specified that procedures would be established whereby the town would pay penalties to the county if the town should later amend the policies to increase densities that adversely affect county budgets.

The idea for these development policies originated in the town's earlier proposal to give the county a role in land use policymaking through separate negotiations. In a sense the town's strategist in the negotiation, the town manager, was now developing the intent signaled earlier in the negotiations. The town was thus refining an existing offer, but to a degree that conveyed to the county team a shift in position. In essence, the town proposed to develop land use policy jointly with the county and to provide sanctions against itself if at a future date the town, in its own interest, unilaterally altered those policies. This proposal gave the county negotiators a viable means to affect land use policy around the town, even though the land would be under town control. Being able to affect that emerging development pattern was one of the county's important goals, and the town offer was crafted to appeal to the county's requirements on the land use control issue.

The mediator assisted the town in developing its offer by discussing with the county staff the county's land use policy requirements, then making the town manager aware of these requirements. The town's formal offer for joint development policies included these two key ideas: (1) that the town would acquire school sites and other public facility sites for the county as development proceeded and (2) that the town would pay an excess development fee should the town allow higher residential densities than originally agreed upon between the parties. These points had originated in the mediator's conversations with the county staff over the past weeks. The mediator had then suggested them to the town in private meetings; the mediator had represented the points as his own proposals. The town included these points as specific inducements to the county, to give the county negotiators a rationale to agree to the major single-stage annexation.

The county caucused after listening to the town proposal. On return to the joint meeting, it expressed willingness to negotiate further on the special development policy concept—as the town's proposal was called—providing certain conditions were accepted. These conditions were (1) that the county's phased annexation approach would be reconsidered if the negotiations faltered on the town approach, (2) that the land issue was not yet considered settled (the town would have to contract its proposed boundaries), and (3) that the town's proposed ten-year moratorium on city status was rejected and the county's proposal for a thirty-year moratorium remained on the table.

After a short discussion about the development policies, the parties caucused to review the offers on the table. On returning from its caucus, the town accepted the county's conditions; thus, both sides agreed to use the town's most recent formal proposal as the framework for further negotiations. Specifically, the county had agreed to withdraw the phased annexation concept in favor of the town's proposal for a significant single-stage annexation, with land management policy jointly developed by the two governments.

While the county team reviewed the new negotiating framework, the town manager used the caucus period to review a new proposal on the land and the city moratorium issues with his negotiators. Once back in joint session, the county accepted the town's approach to settling the issues. Because the county's conditions for acceptance were not onerous, the town negotiators decided the timing was right to offer new concessions on the land and the moratorium issues. The town's strategy at this point was to respond positively and quickly to the county's acceptance of the town's proposal so that the town could create a sense of gain for the county that would induce it to reciprocate by agreeing to the conciliary terms offered, and thus be led to settlement. The town's new proposal had two major elements. First, it moved the proposed annexation line to parallel more closely the ULL, with the exception of the airport. Second, it raised the town's offer from ten to twenty years on its renunciation of city status. Thus, the town negotiators met the county's acceptance of a town proposal to annex a large territory of county land by immediately reciprocating with a counteroffer that might meet the county's conditions of compromise on the annexation line and the number of years that the town would renounce its right to convert to city status.

At ths point both sides saw that an agreement on the amount of land issue was very near and that the other issues, particularly the number of years for the city status moratorium and the details of the joint development policies, could quickly follow. In fact, the agreement on the land and city status moratorium issues was forthcoming, after some competitive bargaining, within the next two negotiating sessions. The other issues were far from settled, however, and the effort to negotiate those issues quickly led to a more polarized and confrontational stage in the negotiations.

Phases 3 and 4:
Confrontation and Agreement Seeking

On July 27, 28, and 29, after weeks of formal proposals, negotiators from both Leesburg and from Loudoun County reached basic agreements on what had been to that point the two key issues in their dispute: the amount of land to be annexed and a moratorium on the town becoming a city. To reach these agreements the negotiating teams employed a structure of detailed formal proposals and counterproposals that focused the parties on the substantive issues. New patterns of interaction and negotiation were necessary, however, as new issues emerged to challenge the parties' commitment to the negotiations. In this section the settlement of the two key issues, the emergence of these new issues, and the patterns of negotiation they generated are described.

In this phase of the negotiation, two types of negotiation behavior—adversarial confrontation and joint problem solving—emerged almost simultaneously in separate negotiating environments, with the same actors involved in each type of interaction. Within six weeks after the beginning of this phase, after the negotiations had nearly broken down twice, the parties signed a comprehensive "Memorandum of Agreement," that later evolved into the final settlement document.

Narrowing Differences

This new phase in the negotiations began on July 27 when the county negotiators accepted the town's proposal, thereby establishing a framework for a negotiated settlement. As the county considered the town's offer both in caucus as soon as it was presented and again after the negotiating session in a more relaxed setting, two themes surfaced. First, the county negotiators felt relieved that the weight of negative and often frustrating negotiations was lifted with the town's offer of a proposal the county probably could accept, a settlement offer that did not appear weighted to the county's disadvantage when compared to the potential settlements in annexation court. Thus, there was a mood of satisfaction among the county team and a sense of having achieved a positive outcome from a difficult position in the negotiation.

The staff immediately began strategizing on how best to further the county's objectives within the context of the new framework for the negotiation (annexation coupled with joint land use development policies). The key substantive issues still appeared to be the location of the boundary line and the length of the moratorium on the town's possible conversion to city status. The county decided to make counterproposals simultaneously aimed at extending the number of years of the moratorium and reducing the proposed land area to be annexed so it would conform to the boundary established by the county's ULL. In the next negotiating session on the following evening, July 28, the county again acknowledged its acceptance of the town's framework for settlement, but requested the town to exclude the Leesburg Airport from its proposal and to extend the moratorium from twenty to twenty-five years. The town initially refused to accede to either request. It insisted that the airport, financially supported and serviced by the town, should be included within the town's new borders and that since it had already extended the moratorium on city status ten years from its earlier proposal, the town had no reason to extend the time limit again. And they acknowledged they were unable to extend it because the town council had not authorized them to consider a moratorium longer than twenty years.

The parties seemed stuck at an impasse—the county demanding at least a twenty-five-year moratorium on city status and a boundary line redrawn to exclude the Leesburg Airport, and the town negotiators indicating they couldn't consider the former and wouldn't consider the latter. They insisted on retaining the airport within their annexed land.

As the two sides reviewed the issue in caucuses, the mediator listened to their conversations and realized that neither side at this point was willing to concede on either issue. Calling the parties back to the negotiating table, the mediator requested each team to meet with its governing board to review the situation and to gain endorsements of the outline for settlement that the teams had agreed to, barring the two remaining issues. The parties agreed to do this. Then the county team members made a specific request: that the town council consider the county's request for a twenty-five year moratorium on city status. The town negotiators agreed to put this issue before the full council. Then the meeting adjourned; no mention was made of the county's position on the airport.

The next evening the town manager began the negotiations with a statement that the council had met and considered the county request and would agree to the twenty-five-year moratorium if the county agreed to include the airport within the town limits. The county team, after a short caucus, accepted this proposal. The issues of the future boundaries of the town and the length of a voluntary moratorium on the town's conversion to a city were basically settled—only minor consensual changes were forthcoming in the next few weeks. The town was to annex just over seven square miles, a little more than half the fifteen square miles it had sought prior to negotiations.

Joint Problem Solving

The town's negotiators next began to piece the agreement together. The manager put forward a two-page list of subjects titled "Annexation Agreement Outline," which was the first written text summarizing the agreement reached by the parties. The list addressed fifteen issues and outlined the town's view of the status and conditions of agreement for each. The first listed item was "Territory," the town's main concern, and it was accompanied by the comment "as agreed." Next on the list was the moratorium issue, combined with an issue new to the talks— the immunity statutes whereby a county can impose permanent town status on a town.

The list continued with the other issues the parties had raised during the period of formal written proposals and counterproposals. These issues, for the most part, were subordinate to the main annexation, city status, and county immunity concerns and had been raised initially in response to mediator's injunction early in the negotiations to identify significant concerns that might be addressed in the process of fashioning settlement to the annexation issue. In discussions over the previous two months, the parties occasionally picked up the thread of one of these issues and reached an understanding on it. That is, as the parties disputed the major differences in their positions on the annexation issues, occasionally grounds for agreement on the subsidiary issues emerged.

In particular, the parties discussed agreements on such issues as the extent of the town's subdivision and utility jurisdiction in the county, the continuation of the town as the county seat, the extension of the town's cable TV franchise development to the annexed area, a new policy on a town-owned solid waste landfill site in the county, and town contributions to the county jail and prosecutor. These verbal understandings were recorded in the "Annexation Agreement Outline."

The introduction of this outlined list of agreements had an important effect on the county negotiators. The county attorney, sensing that both sides could be brought to settlement, began a new role in the negotiations as the drafter of settlement documents. Within twenty-four hours after seeing the town's outline, he had drafted and conveyed to the town a lengthy point-by-point review of it, indicating where the county team agreed with the town's characterization of an issue and where differences remained to be negotiated. On nine of the town's fifteen points the county agreed with the town's statements on the issues; thus those issues were settled. (Formal language needed to be added, however, and these nine agreements were incorporated into the settlement document over two months later!)

In moving toward a single, written text, the parties made a critical procedural breakthrough in the negotiations. The agreements on the individual issues had, of course, evolved over the long span of past negotiating sessions to the point where the written text could be compiled. Once the text was compiled, it served to focus the parties on settlement. The written text clarified for the parties where they were in the negotiations, how much they had achieved, and how much would be lost if the negotiation foundered.

Within two more days, by August 2, the county attorney developed a multi-page, first-draft "Memoranda of Understanding"—a reiteration of earlier written documents and embellished with the most recent perspectives from the negotiating table. This document was succeeded within three days by a second draft, which established many of the legal constructs and much of the language of the final settlement document. The county attorney thus adopted the role of a settlement attorney, a technical resource for both sides and a role that became even more significant when the parties were actually ready to settle the dispute.

The text-drafting process involved review of the county attorney's initial drafts by the town manager and the town's special annexation counsel. Thus, a new setting was created for the negotiation—small meetings of professional staff working through compromises on the issues. As long as the major initiating issues of the annexation boundary and the town's possible city status had remained unresolved, the charged political environment kept the staffs from treating the issues as legal and managerial subjects to be worked through with professional techniques. However, once the breakthrough was made on those key political issues, the staffs began to meet with the mediator, then to work through the necessary compromises. As the rapid introduction of draft settlement agreements indicated, the staffs of both sides, freed from the confines of the formal negotiation, made rapid progress in codifying the agreements reached in earlier discussions.

The agreement-seeking process had first seemed to be well underway at the joint meeting on July 29th when the parties agreed to three significant objectives: (1) to ask the state's Commission on Local Government for a delay in their scheduled September 7 public hearing on the formal annexation case (thus signifying an intention of achieving a negotiated settlement), (2) to produce a signed, final "Memorandum of Understanding" by the end of August, and (3) to work on the language of the joint land development policies, which the county saw as an integral and fundamental part of the agreement. The settlement framework was thus established, and the progress subsequently made in drafting the elements of agreement seemed to indicate that the major disputes had been resolved.

Confrontation

An agreement appeared imminent until a new issue surfaced. This new issue quickly dominated the negotiation because it dealt with a concern underlying the agreements on the land and the moratorium issues—namely, the concern that within several years the county would have sufficient population to permanently bar the town from converting to a city. This immunity issue, like the annexation and city status issues, was associated with a state statute that established particular rights and relations between local governments. The issue did not surface earlier in the negotiations because the town was not concerned over it earlier, and the county saw the issue as a trump card to be played only later in the negotiation. As soon as the boundary issue was settled and the city status moratorium agreed to, the town introduced the immunity issue as part of the settlement equation.

The Immunity Dispute: Mediator Intervention. The town's consideration of the county's immunity rights began when the mediator suggested to the town manager that certain state statutes might substantively affect the town's future right to become a city. The town had carefully bargained before agreeing to a twenty-five-year moratorium on becoming a city and made clear early on that it absolutely refused to permanently renounce its right to ever become a city. Nonetheless, the immunity statutes would allow the county, within ten years, to render the town immune from utilizing the statutory allowance by which towns become cities. In other words, the county would have the option of imposing permanent town status on Leesburg.

The mediator introduced this point to the town on the grounds that one test for an agreement is whether it can be implemented and whether it takes full account of the equities created by its conditions. To test in this way, the parties would have to share knowledge about external conditions that could substantively affect settlement conditions. The immunity statutes worked to the county's advantage in negotiations over the town's moratorium on becoming a city. Earlier in the negotiations, when the mediator had requested the county staff to introduce the issue to the talks, the negotiators had demurred, suggesting it was premature to do so. The county strategists felt the mediator's request would compromise their bargaining position, their resources for influencing the town on future points. When at the point of developing the initial "Memoranda of Understanding," the county still declined to introduce the issue to the town, the mediator introduced it. After checking with their attorney, the town negotiators saw a vital interest at stake and included, at this late stage in the negotiation, a requirement for an agreement on county immunity rights as a complement to the town moratorium. The county staff later indicated that its negotiators had indeed planned to raise the issue and incorporate it into the settlement. By going to the town directly and, in effect, forcing the county's hand on this issue, the county negotiators felt the mediator had somewhat undercut their ability to negotiate effectively in the final stages of the negotiation.

Once introduced to the negotiations, the immunity issue quickly led to an impasse, even though the negotiators had already developed agreements on most of the issues through the process of offering proposals and drafting the text. In fact, the impasse occurred on the same day that the negotiating teams were to review the second draft of the "Memoranda of Understanding" that addressed settlement of all the previous issues.

Both parties saw the immunity issue as crucial to their independent powers of government, and they took unambiguous and opposed positions, indicating they would not compromise principles over the issue. The town stated that it was prepared to return to the litigation process, to give up on the negotiations over this issue. The county suggested that they defer discussion of the issue and move ahead with the negotiations, in particular with the joint request to delay the state's hearing on the original adversarial annexation petition. The town negotiators, however, after conferring with town council, refused to request a delay in the state hearing until the immunity issue was negotiated.

The county insisted that a delay in the state's hearing process was absolutely necessary if the county was to participate in further negotiations. The county must choose, its negotiators stated, either to commit itself to a negotiated settlement or to break off negotiations and put its staff to work preparing an adversarial case for the state commission's hearing. The town, however, remained adamant in their refusal to grant the delay until the immunity issue was settled. Then, the parties decided to take a week off so the town could consult a special counsel to try and find a way to resolve the impasse. The delay of the state's proceedings was not requested and the county left the negotiating table suggesting the clock was running out on the negotiations.

Threats and Compromises. Over the next two weeks the mediator met separately with each negotiating team and conducted other meetings with both the town manager and county attorney present to try and find a way around the immunity dispute. One proposed idea was that both governing bodies jointly approach the state legislature to get new legislation tailored to authorize the parties' agreements and to enable the town and county to protect their respective forms of government. The annexation agreement would reconcile both the county's right to file for immunity and the town's right to file to become a city after the moratorium expires. This idea appealed to the parties, but it still required them to come to agreement on the juxtaposition of the twenty-five-year moratorium on city status for the town and the county's right, within a decade, to prevent the town from ever becoming a city. The issue was complicated because the county, for reasons unrelated to Leesburg, would not consider voluntarily giving up its right to declare itself immune from future annexations and town to city transitions.

In the afternoon prior to the next negotiating session, the chairman of the county board of supervisors, who was a member of the county negotiating team, sent a letter to Leesburg's mayor, a member of the town negotiating team. The letter was a strategic move by the county, an attempt to force its position on the town. The letter, approved by the county's governing board, staked out a position intended to convey that the county negotiators had no discretion over the issue. The letter proposed resolving the issue by suggesting that the county would take steps to preserve the town's right to initiate the process to become a city.

The county proposed that the county would not use its right to become immune from new annexations or from towns becoming cities without first giving Leesburg the right to proceed with its own petition for transition to city status. In other words, the county would not try legally to foreclose the town's existing rights under the law. Specifically, the county suggested that after twenty-five years (the length of the negotiated moratorium on the town's becoming a city) the town would have one year in which to file to become a city. After that year had expired, in 2010, if the town had not filed to become a city, then the county could file for immunity, forever foreclosing the town's option to become a city.

The chairman of the county board coupled this proposal with the demand that the town agree immediately to request a delay in the state commission's hearing process. He then noted that the full board of supervisors had met on the immunity issue for an evening and had formally approved this proposal.

In addition to the technical proposal, the letter contained an implicit sanction (although the county spokesman asked the town to downplay its meaning). The letter stated that because the state commission's reporting deadline was approaching, "unless an extension [delay] is agreed to, the county will be forced to take all steps possible to obtain an extension on its own . . . this may necessitate the filing of a lawsuit . . . [which] would make a return to the negotiation table extremely difficult."

The discussions between the teams in the next negotiating session were difficult and punctuated by caucuses in which the teams separately discussed various options including quitting the negotiations. Feeling that they were losing control of the situation, the parties spoke openly about their concerns and about the forced separation of their positions caused by the conflicting rights in two state statutes. The county again stressed the necessity to request a delay in the state's proceedings. In one tension-filled caucus, the town considered leaving the negotiations; but ultimately, after urging by the mediator, the mayor decided to present a proposal that the town would agree to request the delay if the county would agree fully to protect the town from an immunity filing for the length of the moratorium (twenty-five years) plus one additional year. The proposal also required that the agreement had to be ratified by the state's general assembly—that is, new legislation would be sought to validate the agreement. The county asked for time to consider the proposal, but since it closely paralleled their own they were ready to accept it.

The negotiators met the next day in an unusual daytime meeting. The county was prepared to accept the town proposal from the previous evening, but then the mayor expressed his concern that one year was insufficient time for the town to decide if it wanted to become a city. He reasoned that because the town would be forced to decide, it would almost inevitably choose to exercise its option while it could. He also indicated concern that the town negotiating team had gone further than the council had authorized them on this issue. He needed to get back to the council and ask them to authorize continuing this line in the talks.

Four days later the negotiating teams met again. This negotiating session was the only one the mediator did not attend and this fact affected the conduct of the meeting. Prior to this meeting the town had proposed by letter a new approach to the immunity issue—an open-ended commitment by the county not to seek permanent immunity and thus foreclose the town's transition options. The county negotiators indicated that their governing board, the board of supervisors, had considered the proposal and rejected its terms. They counteroffered a two-year time period within which the town might file to become a city.

The town manager rejected this offer and reminded the county that no request for a delay, which the county insisted must be forthcoming, would be made unless this issue was resolved. The county administrator repeated the offer for a two-year time period; another county official suggested that the county might consider some alternative time period.

After further discussions, which included some explicit threats by the county to take adversarial actions if the negotiations collapsed, the two teams fell into long silences. One silence lasted more than thirty minutes— the two negotiating teams were simply trying to outwait each other. At one point the town manager noted that the problem seemed to escape solution that evening and asked, "Do we book another meeting, or not?"

Later when another statement was made that the town perceived as a threat, the town manager suggested ending the meeting. The county, however, had every intention of settling the issue that night if it possibly could. After further discussion, the town manager asked the county team to reconsider its offer on the time period. After a caucus the county responded with a proposal for a four-year time period. The town held out for a five-year period and the county agreed, provided a letter requesting the delay in the state commission hearing was signed that evening. The town accepted, the letter was signed, and the immunity-delay issue was resolved.

Settlement

Resolution of the impasse over the immunity issue marked the end of the last major dispute threatening the negotiated settlement. Yet settlement was far from a certainty; other disputes remained that had the potential to disrupt the settlement process. The parties' strong commitment to settlement made settlement more likely though. Actual settlement demanded that the staffs of the town and county work intensively within a tight timeframe to overcome their remaining differences, that they draft settlement documents acceptable to both negotiating teams and the governing boards, and that they draft state legislation to support the agreement and then successfully market that legislation to important interest groups and state legislators. These tasks were not simple and required impressive commitment by the town and county staffs, which was forthcoming. The county attorney and the town manager communicated to their staffs the overall benefits of the negotiated settlement, which the county attorney and the town manager recognized even though they were working through issues point by point in sometimes difficult negotiations.

Although the parties had agreed, prior to the immunity dispute, on a broad outline for joint policies governing land development in the area to be annexed, they had yet to work through the practical details of those policies. The joint policies were an essential part of the overall agreement; they included issues representing some of the most basic town-county conflicts during the dispute. Negotiation of the joint development policies was the most significant remaining task. The parties also had to finish the "Memorandum of Understanding," the basic settlement document. This document had been through two drafts when discussion on it was suspended because of the rise of the immunity dispute.

Immediately following resolution of the immunity dispute on August 24, the town and county staffs began work on the language of the final "Memorandum of Understanding," then on the joint development policies, and then on the first draft for language for state legislation to support the agreement. On August 30 the full negotiating teams met to review the necessity for legislation, the outline of the memorandum, and the joint development policies. Although the parties were dealing with the substance of the settlement, the tone of their exchanges at that meeting resumed an adversarial character. The parties had entered the final stage of the negotiation, and this knowledge made them, particularly the town's negotiators, conservative rather than conciliatory because they realized they had fewer opportunities to configure the settlement to their advantage.

During the following week the county attorney and the town manager exchanged and reviewed drafts of the memorandum, narrowing the list of issues to be reviewed in a final, joint negotiating session. On September 9, the negotiating teams reviewed in detail the memorandum to finalize their agreements on the substantive issues (except the joint land development policies, which remained to be negotiated). This meeting required compromises on some points that had been generally resolved earlier. There were difficulties and tensions in the meeting as the parties contested certain points and as compromises were made. In general, the county team was the more conciliatory one at this stage in the negotiations. The county team found the final form of the agreement preferable to the prospect of litigation over the annexation; thus it was prepared to go along with minor adjustments in the document as long as the major points of the agreement were not importantly affected. The town team, particularly the manager and the mayor, felt more circumspect about the agreement than they had earlier; they felt they might well have achieved from the court the land boundary they had negotiated without the attendant strings of the land development policy. Yet they were supporting the agreements reached, and they did not at all want to back out of the agreements. Since they did not feel it incumbent upon them to be as conciliatory as they had been earlier, they raised and fought for the points that they wanted in the settlement document. The county responded with accommodations.

After four hours of review by paragraph-by-paragraph analysis and occasional haggling, the negotiators agreed on the final contents of the "Memorandum of Understanding." They agreed to meet four days later to sign it. The ten-page document established the bases for the settlement, the actions each governing body was to take to reach settlement, and the conditions of settlement—the agreements on thirteen intergovernmental issues that when adopted by the governing boards and ratified by the state and court would settle the dispute.

The negotiations were still not over. The staffs of the county and town—particularly the county attorney, the county planning staff, and the town manager—spent the next six weeks drafting the joint land development policies as an attachment to the formal agreement. The county proposed that the policies should be detailed and supported with policy descriptions and analyses. The town manager suggested a tighter design: simple statements of the applicable policies. Although these stylistic differences exacerbated the negotiations over the relatively minor substantive differences that remained, negotiations were not threatened by failure because the parties at this point were fully committed to the settlement agreements they already had initialed. The town manager and county attorney were now negotiating over a narrow range of issues. Even so, as the drafts of the joint land development policies document were reviewed new issues surfaced that required mutual adjustments.

Finally, on November 1, 1982, almost six months after the beginning of formal negotiations, the town and county announced the following: their formal agreement on the negotiated annexation of some seven square miles by the town; the commitment by both sides to a twenty-six page set of joint policies guiding land development in the area to be annexed; detailed agreements on city status, immunity, and structural relations between the town and county over the next twenty-five years; and numerous other interlocal issues. The negotiated settlement had been difficult and expensive. The range and quality of this settlement was much richer than the settlement a statutory and court-based process could have produced.

Two weeks later, after public hearings on the agreement and after citizen comments were reviewed, the Loudoun County Board of Supervisors and the Leesburg Town Council adopted the modified "Memorandum of Agreement" and joint development policies as the formal agreement between the two governments that ended the annexation dispute.

Review and Conclusions

This case indicates a valid role for formal negotiation processes in certain intergovernmental disputes. The case used a structured negotiation managed by a third-party mediator as an alternative to litigation to settle an important jurisdictional dispute. That the structured negotiation environment stimulated new forms of negotiation between the parties that enabled them to work through their adversarial positions to reach an overall settlement is clearly demonstrated by the details of the case.

The structured negotiation, a formal process that included teams of local officials and a mediator, supported the emergence of intrateam and interteam dynamics that came to dominate the negotiation process. Given these dynamics, the concept of negotiation as a rational process of positional bidding turned out to be of only limited use to the parties. This traditional model of rational bargaining strategy was used by the parties at the initiation of the negotiations and occasionally throughout the talks. However, the parties found themselves influenced as much by the affective content of the issues as by abstract calculations of their positions. For example, they were much influenced by meanings communicated to them, by their personal reactions to what they heard and individualistic interpretations of their opponent's positions and statements. This deep involvement in one another's statements affected not only each party's views of its opponent's interests but also each party's perception of the willingness of its opponent to address seriously its own concerns.

The parties engaged in both confrontive behaviors and problem-solving behaviors at different points within the negotiation. The negotiations process was initiated by the third-party mediator. The structure and norms of the process conditioned the parties' actions thereby creating a setting within which the negotiation dynamics could be safely worked out—that is, creating opportunities for controlled exchanges and a setting conducive to negotiating a settlement.

A Setting for Intergovernmental Mediation

The structured negotiations process of this case is a new, alternative approach to interjurisdictional dispute resolution. This approach depends upon external support from legislative, administrative, and judicial authorities to gain legitimacy with public-sector disputants. There would have been no structured negotiation for this particular dispute without initial advocacy for the process by the state agency with jurisdiction in such disputes. The experiences of the parties in this case and of the parties in other, similar cases leads us to speculate that in interjurisdictional disputes in which (1) organized negotiation procedures are set forth by statute as an alternative to litigation, (2) the state agencies that supervise such statutes encourage the use of negotiating structures, and (3) negotiated settlements can be made binding, structured negotiations processes will be employed with increasing frequency. In disputes lacking such statutory or state administrative support, however, the processes will remain unused—unsupported, unfamiliar processes will not be introduced in conflict settings with high stakes.

An important characteristic of the negotiations process represented by this case is that because it is a new and formalized type of intergovernmental negotiation, it creates interaction dynamics among public officials that are different from the traditional intergovernmental interactions that accompany litigation or administrative or political bargaining. These new channels for interaction and the dynamics that surface through the negotiation context can, as demonstrated in this case, add dimensions to intergovernmental management. That lesson is the real contribution of the case. Identification of some of the major points of that lesson follows.

Why Formal Negotiations?

Could negotiations have worked if they were less formally structured, that is, if they were without the services of an outside mediator? In this case the parties had attempted to establish direct negotiations during the year preceding the town's formal action for annexation; they had managed only a few isolated meetings, and these were useful for stating positions and not for establishing a negotiation process. During these aborted sessions the parties reinforced an existing negative sense of each other's objectives. Each side was perceived (by its opponent) as aggressively pursuing policies harmful to its opponent. An added complication in late 1981 was the palpable friction between the professional staffs of the two localities, which made the establishment of lasting direct negotiations unlikely.

In the end the parties came to the negotiating table because the statute addressing the annexation process included a provision that either party could compel the other to enter negotiations and, consequently, suspend normal actions before the state agency for a period of sixty days. The town initiated the petition and suspected the county would compel the negotiations. The town wanted to proceed with its case so it endorsed the negotiations process to get that imminent delay (imminent in the town's view) over with. The town was quite pessimistic about the county's willingness to cede significant land areas through any process short of a judicial order. The county was also pessimistic about the prospects of a negotiated settlement; yet it was willing to enter formal talks in the hope that the town's position would become more reasonable as a result of the talks and that, consequently, an accommodation could be worked out. Had the process not been strongly recommended by the state agency initially hearing the town's annexation petition, it is quite likely that the town would not have entered formal negotiations because it wanted the process over with as soon as possible and thought the courts were the quickest process.

The presence of an independent mediator was necessary in this case to reorganize the negotiation effort as a formal process with its own set of participants and rules. Since certain other localities had been facing similar issues, these parties might have been able to establish a structure for negotiations without a mediator had they not had the experience of their previous tentative and aborted direct negotiations. That experience convinced the parties that their opponents were willing to negotiate only on different premises and with different negotiation goals. Therefore, a mediator was thought necessary—as one negotiator later put it, "a stranger in the midst causes everyone to be more polite."

The mediator performed an essential role at the outset by providing a neutral context, a context in which the parties could bring their initial positions to the bargaining table without immediately causing a breakdown of the talks. Given the state of their relations in the early spring of 1982, these parties probably would not have been able to sustain the negotiations process without a mediator. Through the first two months of the process, each party was determined to attain very different settlements and each was convinced that the opponent was not willing to accept its own requirements for a negotiated settlement. At the level of positioning on the issues, and at the level of interteam dynamics, the parties saw only intractable and negative opponents. Without the mediator's interventions in the first weeks of the negotiations, the talks almost inevitably would have broken down. Formal negotiations led by a third-party neutral most likely were necessary through at least the midpoint in the negotiations.

The Evolution of a Complex Negotiation

Negotiation of this case was earlier described as comprising four phases: exploration and strategy formulation, formal proposals, confrontation, and agreement seeking. Evolutionary stages in a joint activity are expected; groups coming together to accomplish a task typically go through changes as they learn to work together. The phases described in this and the companion case study, however, have emerged from the close observation of negotiation participants engaged in adversarial relations, not supportive relations common in joint endeavors. The phases therefore mark the evolution of the joint enterprise between adversaries. These phases are not conclusions based on a priori models of the negotiation process; these phases were observed among negotiators at different stages in a real negotiation. A spectrum of intergovernmental mediation cases have also exhibited this same sequence of negotiating behaviors. The phases represent different levels of interteam and, significantly, intrateam development of the issues, as well as each side's approach to the negotiation. The phases, that is, mark the character of intrateam and interteam dynamics prevailing at a given stage in the negotiation. The phases, or status of the negotiation at a point in time, indicate how individual negotiators are perceiving the negotiation as a whole. The perceptions of individual members are, of course, influenced by their sense of their own role in the negotiation, their view of how the issues affect their personal stakes and the public interests they represent, the dynamics of intrateam exchanges, and individual and team interactions with the opposing negotiators.

The parties in this case spent the majority of the negotiation (perhaps 95 percent) dealing with their opponents in unilaterally determined adversarial activities—positioning themselves, reacting to positions, and repositioning. Even in most of the positive, productive negotiation sessions, the parties could be characterized as working in unilateral and confrontational settings. The negotiations bore little resemblance to a joint process until the parties passed through several evolutionary phases of the environment that supported the fashioning of a settlement. At that late point, the parties moved easily and quickly into the context of a joint process. The joint process was characterized by relatively open communication channels—the parties exchanged concepts and fashioned agreements without undue defenses against attack and loss of position. Until the parties reached a common understanding of the problems in settling their dispute, they worked separately and spent much of their time castigating the other side, attacking its motives and its participants' sincerity about negotiations.

Obviously, much of what happens in a complex negotiation involves unplanned, nonstrategic behavior. The disputants typically spend a good portion of time forming strategies on how to get the other side to accept their premises or proposals, but usually strategies of this sort are lost on opponents who are also committed to an adversarial posture. These strategies may, however, successfully provide the team initiating as proposed with an opportunity to gain knowledge and perspective on the issues. As the parties gain perspective on the issues, new options may emerge. The process of considering options tends to increase options; most of this important work must be done within a team, in intrateam negotiations. It is by looking for options and determining positions, which often turn out to be more flexible than individuals earlier believed, that participants open themselves to new formulations. An attitude recognizing the utility of new options may lead to lowered resistance to proposals put forward by the other side, thereby moving the parties to the joint problem-solving phase.

One observed phenomenon in this case study and in other cases is both parties' retreating from the clear path to an agreement at a late stage in joint problem solving. In this case that phase, which emerged after an agreement on the annexation territory was reached, was labeled the confrontation phase. In the accompanying case (Virginia City–Oceanside County) the same phase was labeled the return to competitive bargaining phase. In both of these cases, after months of confrontational bargaining and brinkmanship, the parties moved to new ground and laid out the outlines of a settlement. Then, between joint meetings, the parties each became more adverse to risk and less willing to engage in open problem solving; they even discussed taking a hard-line position on an issue and demanding that the other side accede to that position. They wanted proof of the opponent's good faith in light of the major compromises already made from the initial negotiating position.

The confrontation after the Leesburg-Loudoun land issue was settled centered around each party's commitment to maintain its separate advantage under state statutes that governed the town's future right to become a city and the county's future right to prevent such a town action. The issue itself was a crucial one to each party. In this confrontational phase, as at this phase in other disputes, the parties' reactions to the surfacing of a tough issue and to each other's positions was similar to negotiating behaviors in an earlier phase in the negotiations—the adversarial strategy formation phase. The parties soon locked into a confrontational relationship, using adversarial strategies to try and compel their opponents to adopt their position.

Reviewing the situation we are led to speculate that because the joint negotiation process was laboriously constructed over a given set of issues and over an extended time period, the parties became very familiar with both the issues and their opponents' positions and interests. That familiarity made it safe to move from a protective adversarial context to a position of making more flexible proposals and of receiving proposals without the need to reject them out of hand. The initial positive move from confrontation to problem solving was limited to the specific major issues of the negotiation. The joint process established to manage the original major issues might not have been able to contain the new issues that emerged near the end of the negotiations. (This hypothesis not only explains why the return to open problem solving and discussion involved particular major issues but why the confrontation recurred.)

The elaboration of the phases in a negotiation thus have functional meaning. They identify some of the architectural elements of a long and complicated negotiation. The phases describe behavioral stages through which adversarial disputants must pass to reach settlement. What is particularly important is that the phases mark stages of interteam and intrateam dynamics, the evolving uneven state of communications among the participants in the negotiation.

The Mediation Role

The mediator in this case undertook various roles as the conditions of the negotiation changed. He entered the dispute as the neutral organizer and manager of the negotiations process, serving as the facilitator of joint meetings and, occasionally, of intrateam negotiations. His experience with the same issues in other cases helped him to serve the parties as a technical consultant on the substantive issues. He relayed to each side his sense of the other side's feelings about the state of the negotiation. Late in the negotiations he became active in the formulation of positions by one or the other parties by conveying information between the teams. In caucuses he worked to maintain the negotiations process by responding with discussions, reviews, and counterpoints to keep the parties within the structure of the negotiations.

Three mediator roles can be clearly drawn from this case: (1) designer and manager of the negotiation, (2) process facilitator in the negotiating sessions, and (3) intervenor affecting the design of substantive positions on the issues in caucus sessions with the parties. We will consider each in turn.

Negotiation Designer. This is the primary role for the third party in disputes at an impasse—the point at which parties distrust each other. The parties in this case had their own strongly held ideas on how the negotiations should be conducted, and each side was initially determined not to give the appearance of conceding on this issue. Finding an impasse on the organizational issue, the mediator immediately took a strong line, specifying to each side in separate meetings his expert opinion on how the negotiations should be structured. His purpose in asserting a single best way to set up the negotiations was twofold: (1) to cut through the thicket of each side's rejection of the other's approach to the negotiation and establishing a process that he felt would work well for the parties and (2) to establish clearly his own role as an authoritative neutral actor in the negotiation.

The mediator's first act—after an initial joint meeting with the parties' representatives at which he was formally designated as the mediator—

was to meet separately with the full governing bodies of the two communities to establish those bodies, and not any other representatives, as his clients. His objective was to widen the participation in the negotiation, to bring elected officials directly into the flow of the talks, and to ascertain the relationships between the overall boards and their negotiating teams. Had he found incongruities between a team's perception of the issues and those of its full board, he would have resolved those differences before moving to the joint meeting process.

During these early interviews the mediator asked one side to reconstitute its negotiating team to include elected officials. At that time the composition of the teams was an issue between the parties. One side had appointed a team without elected officials by formal resolution, the other team insisted that negotiations must include elected officials. The mediator, meeting separately with each side, asserted his own views based on past experience and set forth his proposal for the makeup of the negotiating teams, as well as other matters about the conduct of the negotiations. Both sides agreed to his formulation of the structure and makeup of the negotiation teams and the broad process for negotiations.

In his initial meetings with each side, the mediator tried to confer a sense of formal structure and legitimacy to the negotiations process. He proposed that the parties meet at a neutral site, that they tentatively schedule several sessions, that they employ a formal, joint meeting-caucus model, that he have access to caucuses, and that a negotiation agreement be signed by all participants specifying their consent not to use any offers or statements made in the negotiations in any other forum. In addition, the mediator explained he would encourage each party to develop formal proposals and counterproposals addressing a variety of issues. His objective in these early moves was to establish a sense that these negotiations would be different from what had previously taken place—namely, that these negotiations would provide a new setting and a different and viable process to which the disputants might subscribe without relinquishing commitments to their established positions. His goal was to develop the parties' respect for his role and the parties' confidence that they could participate safely in this negotiation.

Process Interventions. In joint meetings, formal negotiating sessions, and caucuses with each negotiating team, the mediator acted as moderator and process facilitator, intervening in exchanges to help the parties maintain and enhance their communications with each other. Given the evident experience and competence of these participants in managing meetings, the mediator adopted a relatively low profile by design. In the normal flow of negotiations he took a supportive and adaptive role, cautiously intervening where needed in the dynamics of interpersonal, interteam, and intrateam exchanges. The mediator for the most part chose to react to situations as the parties fashioned them; he let the parties define the dynamics of exchange. He would, for example, generally not try to stop the initiation of a negotiation tactic that in his opinion was conceived in a defensive context and was sure to elicit a rejecting response from the other side. Instead he would go over the tactic with the negotiatiors prior to the joint session, asking them to review its probable impacts and try to imagine their reaction if they were on the receiving end of that tactic. When the team persisted in following its original line, he would not stop them from doing so, nor would he try to blunt the impact in any way.

The mediator took the stance that conflict per se was not to be avoided; the parties needed exposure to their opponents' values and interests, even if it meant heated exchanges. The mediator did intervene when the parties came to points of critical communication breakdowns. In these situations he acted to clear communications channels, trying to make sure that the meanings of statements were understood as intended. When such meanings by design or accident generated conflicts between individuals or teams, the mediator intervened only if he judged that the negotiation was being threatened by the exchanges. In general, the mediator adopted a responsive approach to the parties' exchanges, intervening only when he felt the pressure of the immediate situation made it timely and necessary to assist the parties either in communications or in the formulation of certain substantive points for the parties' consideration.

Though limited, the mediator's process interventions were important in maintaining the flow of negotiations over difficult points in which the parties were only marginally interested in keeping the negotiations alive. In a few situations early in the negotiation, and again during the confrontation over the immunity issue, the efforts that the mediator directed toward keeping the negotiations moving may have prevented the breakdown of the process. In cases where tensions were high because of the way team members from one side characterized the other or because of the frustration of dealing with seemingly obdurate opponents, the mediator would refocus the discussion by asking the parties to clarify or restate points; alternatively, he would attempt to sum up a position, thus letting each side take a crack at his formulation rather than attacking each other.

An interesting example of the significance of these process interventions occurred late in the negotiations at the only joint meeting from which the mediator was absent. During this meeting the teams reached an impasse and approximately ten people sat around a table for more than half an hour in silence. The parties were able to overcome this visible impasse on their own (in fact this was orchestrated by just one side) because it came very late in the negotiations after each side was fundamentally convinced that a settlement could be reached. In this case the mediator's absence, known in advance, was used by one side as an opening to use an impasse as a pressure tactic in the negotiation. (It was not markedly successful.)

Issues Involvement. Mediators inevitably are involved in the communication of substantive proposals among the parties in a negotiation. The style of mediator involvement in the issues depends in part on the characteristics of the dispute situation, in particular the dynamics of interteam meetings. In this case, as in many intergovernmental negotiations, the preferred strategy was to have the parties bring their positions to the negotiating table directly and not to have the mediator shuttle back and forth with substantive proposals between separated parties. The process of joint meetings and formal proposals provides a rich context and setting in which each side gives direct feeling-based responses to proposals. (Descriptions of both the reliance on joint meetings and the consequent necessity for developing formal written proposals prior to meetings are found in the section in this chapter entitled "Phase 2: Formal Proposals.") The mediator rejected the artificial separation of the parties, which frees them from dealing with the reactions that proposals can generate; the mediator encouraged the parties to use the joint meeting process as the basic method for exchanging proposals.

The parties did rely primarily on the joint meetings for the exchange of proposals; they sought the mediator's intermediary services in their caucuses. In fact the mediator played two roles in these caucuses. The mediator reviewed the teams' proposals with them, listening for underlying limits, boundaries, and interests; then he conveyed his reactions, his questions and concerns. Each party quizzed the mediator about the other side—for example, they asked what the other side was planning and what was its reaction to the last session. Alternatively, the parties laid out their proposals and justified them to the mediator, demanding the mediator's agreement about the fairness of the proposals.

After weeks of these interviews with each side, both before and after joint meetings, the mediator asked one side, the town, to address an underlying issue. This issue was very important to the county, and the county's position on it was not one the town would accept. After discussions between the mediator and the town negotiators, the town reconfigured its own proposal to address the county's interests. The county then agreed to the town's formulation. At the initiation of the negotiation and for the first month or so thereafter the parties were far apart on this issue. The mediator's private meetings with each side made him aware of the key underlying concern and how to communicate it to the other side in a way that stimulated the development of a counteroffer ultimately acceptable to both sides.

Other instances of mediator involvement in substantive issues involve a higher profile than the one employed in the example just described— for example, situations in which the mediator drafts a text with the parties to summarize their positions and situations in which the mediator prepares a text and offers it as an approach to settling certain issues. This writer has successfully used that approach in intergovernmental negotiations, and it can be most powerful. The low-profile approach is more subtle; it is also more likely to result in an agreement if underlying interests can be identified in private meetings, then communicated as suggestions from the mediator to the other side, then addressed by the other side in its proposal without compromising its position. In this way, the mediator serves the parties by representing one side to the other through a neutral role. Ideas that may be rejected in joint session— simply because their acceptance might, in the parties' view, appear as being too conciliatory (which they assume could hurt them in other stages of the negotiation)—may be acceptable on their merits when communicated by the mediator.

4

The Virginia City–Oceanside County
Boundary Negotiations*

Introduction

Every case involving a policy issue of any scope in public administration is unique or has highly distinctive features, and the Virginia
City-Oceanside County annexation-immunity case is illustrative of this
principle.[1] Although the history of events in the case fit rather nicely
the five-stage model of negotiations introduced in chapter 1—and for
this reason we will use this model as a framework for presenting this
case—the reader will see in it a number of novel and interesting aspects.

The reader will see one such aspect in the fifth stage or agreement
phase, which in this case was particularly delicate and tricky. The
mediator in the case played a more pivotal role than usual in bringing
about the agreement that was ultimately reached. All in all, this case
is perhaps an unusually good example of the many ways that mediators
can have an impact upon intergovernmental disputes.

The Context

The County of Oceanside is venerable for its colonial tradition (it
was founded before 1750), large (over 400 square miles), and rural
(though its population grew rapidly in the 1970s, like most of Virginia's
counties, it still contains fewer than seventy-five persons per square
mile). Most of the significant population concentrations in the county,
moreover, were included within the areas of the annexation-immunity
dispute that is the focus of this case.[2] Also included in these areas were
the major commercial, industrial, and public facilities developments that
the county contains and that give it its identity as a government. The
cultural identity of the county is rather distinctive. About half of its

---

*Virginia City and Oceanside County are fictitious names; no localities in Virginia have
these names.

civilian labor force is employed in nonagricultural wage and salary positions; the other half work either outside the county or in agricultural production. Most of the county is productive agricultural land, and the county contains thousands of acres of commercial forest lands. By contrast, the county has been undergoing rather diversified growth and development in the areas of commerce and industry, and in the decade preceding 1985, nonagricultural employment increased significantly. Hence, the overall pattern in the county is largely one of concentrated population, vacant (that is, forest) land, agricultural activity, and commercial and industrial growth.

It seems justified to characterize the county ethos, created in part by these physical characteristics, as one that centers around traditional rural values of independence, thrift, and minimal government and that is tempered by a practical, businessman's awareness that growth and development are desirable and that effective government complements such development. The county's political leaders see themselves as providing a definitely different *style* of government from the urban centers in the county, and they feel their style is superior to the city style. During the negotiation sessions both sides made regular reference to this rivalry, in varying degrees of jest and seriousness. The county seemed to see itself as capable of governing under essentially urban circumstances, but in a manner that would be both different and more effective than what they saw as characteristic of city government.

Virginia City also has venerable roots in both U.S. and Virginia history. It also was founded in early colonial days and quickly became the center of commerce and development in the county. Its present size is about 12 square miles, which it reached through a series of annexations carried out since it achieved city status in the late nineteenth century.[3] Most of the city's territory was gained in the city's last annexation action, which occurred before 1950. In the 1970s, in common with many of Virginia's smaller cities, Virginia City's population decreased a little but its density still remained high, well over 2,000 persons per square mile. The city had in 1985 less than one square mile of land that was vacant and not constrained from development by environmental factors, and much of this small amount was not suitable for industrial or commercial uses. The city is a central focus of the commercial and civic life of the area, containing major entertainment and shopping areas, the region's courts, and other state agencies and institutions.

As the case narrative will reveal, the attitude of Virginia City toward local government is certainly different from that of the county, if not antithetical to it. The city saw itself as much more in the position of having to respond to a rather urgent and problematic situation of meeting an increasing need and demand for services with a static or dwindling reservoir of resources. Its stance was active and its sense of its situation was concrete—based on what it considered to be an objective and professional assessment of the plain facts. The city did not see itself as attempting to act against the county, but rather responding to a general public interest. To a significant extent, the context in this case is one marked by the encounter between the rural attitude and the urban attitude.

The Negotiation Teams and the Ethos

The contrast just noted was embodied with only minor exception in the membership of the negotiating teams that represented the two parties to the case. The county team was made up of one county supervisor who was elected from a district that would be directly affected by the proposed annexation and another county supervisor from an area not directly affected by it. (The county's special legal counsel recommended such appointment.) Both men were characteristic of the county board of supervisors generally, which was made up of well-to-do farmers and businessmen. In many ways they were urbane and knowledgeable about government events and trends in both the state and nation; nonetheless, they brought to their roles a perspective that was grounded in the earth of Oceanside County—for example, they scheduled negotiation sessions around the timing of farm chores like milking and harvesting.

The two other members of the team, the county administrator and the county attorney, though educated professionals, shared these views and hence, were in their own way professional counterparts of the board membership. Both professed a strong belief in the superiority of life in the country over life in the city, and both showed appreciation for the contribution of the country people in the county to the culture, traditions, and the institutional stability of the area. Both were capable of strong shows of emotion and seemed to view negotiation as involving a certain amount of stylization or ritual—as one associates, for example, with a business deal or a horse trade.

By contrast, the city team had a more urban-professional makeup largely because of its young mayor, who was a local attorney, and its soft-spoken, professionally oriented city manager. Also on the team during the time the mediators were involved in the case was a young corporate manager with an MBA. Even though the city attorney, the fourth member, was somewhat older and a more traditional Virginia City representative, he took a posture that was heavily grounded in his professional role as an attorney. The overall impression that the team gave was markedly more urban than the county team. The degree of the contrast was striking since Virginia City is not large and the city is so much a part of the county and area-wide culture.

Oceanside County's officials felt that the city governments' seeking to annex part of the county was an attempt to use the law to take what was historically and rightly county land. In fact, a perception of relentless encroachment by the city on the county seemed to condition the county's viewpoint from the outset. One of the county's underlying desires (which became an important objective in the negotiation) was to secure a place that it could develop as a symbol and fact of county government—a county seat, in effect—that was safe from future city annexations forever. The county characterized itself as much like the beleaguered American Indian who was encroached upon and who wanted and deserved a reservation of its own. This motive had a large role in creating the case and must be considered a determining force throughout the case—its resolution ultimately hinged on this issue.

Another aspect of the psychology of the county's side was its strong aversion to influences on negotiations wrought by special attorneys for cities—the Richmond lawyers they were called. The county felt that another city's special attorney blocked settlement in a previous annexation case, and this belief colored their talks with Virginia City. Indeed, it was sometimes observed that the county did not manifest a particularly charitable attitude toward its *own* special attorneys. The county would have preferred that local policymaking be restricted to local government officials. They accepted the mediators to the extent that they saw them as working toward this same goal.

Phase 1: Preliminary Explorations

The genesis for the events in this case was a "breakfast committee" made up of administrators and officials from Virginia City and Oceanside County. This committee had been formed as a vehicle for informal contact and information sharing among the the jurisdictions. During one of its meetings representatives from the city mentioned the possibility of moving for annexation as a possible solution to its fiscal difficulties. Apparently, however, this was not brought up as an official possibility, and the county simply acknowledged the mention. However, the county subsequently learned through formal channels that the city council had directed the city manager to open negotiations with the county on the topic of a friendly annexation.

As a result apprehension began to grow among the county leadership about Virginia City's ambitions for annexation, even though the city manager made no immediate move to act on his council's mandate to seek negotiations. It is fitting to note that the mayor of Virginia City, in June 1984,[4] wrote the county administration requesting information relevant to a study of the possibility for economic revenue sharing between the two jurisdictions. The county responded that it would cooperate up to a point, but it wanted to know specifically what the city was seeking. The city, apparently, was seeking to present a friendly demeanor toward the county during this period.

A local newspaper reported that a statement by the mayor had "set a friendly tone." The mayor's statement included "we are now friendly neighbors, let's remain friendly neighbors" and five possible alternatives for resolving the city's problematic situation: (1) economic revenue sharing between the city and county, (2) annexation of a portion of the county by the city, (3) consolidation of the city and county, or a partial consolidation of some governmental functions, (4) more joint ventures and sharing of facilities, and (5) the establishment of a regional government with limited authority. The mayor presented these alternatives in a prepared statement delivered at a dinner on July 23; the county was present, at the city's invitation.

The mayor stressed that at that point the city was open-minded about which alternative was best. Furthermore, a local newspaper reported that the county board was in "complete agreement" with the contents of the mayor's statement. The city council requested informal talks with the county, during which the various approaches could be discussed. The city designated as its representatives for these talks the mayor, another council member, the city manager, and the city attorney. The dinner was characterized by a kind of friendly tentativeness on both sides, with the city actively seeking a cooperative approach to the situation.

Then in late August the county filed for immunity from annexation before the Virginia Commission on Local Government. The immunity petititon meant that the county was requesting that a specifically defined area of land, in this case some twenty-five square miles, would be legally designated as exempt from annexation in perpetuity. The county, in announcing its actions, said that it was acting on the advice of counsel—it named the county attorney, then mentioned that it had retained special counsel in June. The county administrator did stipulate that he hoped negotiations would continue.

The city, in response, said it was shocked and disappointed at the action, having hoped that good-faith negotiations could have led to a plan for resolving the city's problems in cooperation with the county. On September 7 the Virginia City council hired a law firm to represent it in the dispute and allocated over $100,000 for what then seemed to be the imminent battle before the Commission on Local Government and the courts. The informal discussions of the city's five approaches ceased.

At this point the Commission on Local Government, in its continuing informal monitoring of the situation, asked whether the parties wished it to appoint a mediator. Neither of the parties wanted a mediator because they believed that without a mediator they could hold discussions among themselves (using personal persuasion) and because bringing in a mediator at that point would indicate an escalation in the degree of conflict.

At this time, mid-September, Virginia City employed a consulting firm to develop data for its case. The county and city met in Richmond with the commission and agreed to negotiate. The county appointed a team for the negotiations consisting of the county administrator, the county attorney, one board member who represented an area certain to be affected by any possible annexation action, and one whose area would not be so affected.

October and November were rather quiet. There were occasional editorials urging mediation and complaining about the costs of the dispute, but not much interaction occurred between Virginia City and Oceanside County.

On December 10 the city announced to the commission that expansion of its boundaries appeared to be absolutely essential. About a week later the local paper reported that mediation was being considered for the case.

In early January 1985 the commission held four days of hearings on the immunity case, urging all parties to negotiate. Another editorial appeared urging negotiation.

At this point a court that was considering another annexation case announced its decision—it amounted to a rather devastating defeat for the county involved. Just after this announcement, the mayor of Virginia City, whom the county attorney had charged with side-stepping invitations from the county to meet for negotiations, announced that Virginia City was ready to negotiate with Oceanside at the earliest possible date.

After subsequent meetings the city indicated that it needed more information (it had been gathering information) on the annexation alternative before it could decide whether it was the best course. The city did, however, allocate more funds to the case, bringing its total appropriation to almost $300,000. Then in the midst of further meetings, the city on February 19 petitioned to annex a total of eighteen square miles. The county administrator, speaking for the county, said he was "disappointed" in this action and that he "thought the talks were getting somewhere." In mid-March the city presented to the commission its plans for serving the sizable area it was proposing to annex. In early

April the city announced again that it was standing firm on annexation, perhaps provoking the subsequent calls for a negotiated settlement and consolidation from the local chamber of commerce, the county farmers and businessmen's association, and the retail merchants association. Next the council allocated another $200,000 to the case (the reported total was brought to over half a million dollars), which was followed by another editorial urging that a mediator be called in.

Just before Easter the two teams held a series of six joint meetings. Both sides presented outlines of plans for joint revenue sharing and they agreed to ask the commission to appoint a mediator. They felt that a mediator could bring an early settlement.

In initial meetings with the city manager on May 5, the newly appointed mediators learned that the city had some concern over the mediators' past experience even though the city had agreed to the appointments. The city's feeling was that the mediators might possibly pressure them to make concessions to the county against their own interests. The mediators argued that this reasoning was based on a misunderstanding of the mediator's role. They explained that their role was not so much to pressure the sides for concessions as to keep the process of negotiation going well enough and long enough for an agreement to be reached that both sides willingly accepted. They went on to note that one of the advantages of a two-man mediation team was that each mediator could act as a check on the other in watching for bias toward or misperception of the parties to the dispute. Discussion of the matter seemed to dispel this concern to a significant extent.

The initial encounters of the mediators with the teams were primarily for the purpose of becoming familiar with the personalities and group chemistry and to gathering information about the status of the talks. The public pronouncement about bringing in mediators maintained that this action reflected momentum for an agreement, that the parties felt mediators could help make the final push to success. The actual situation seemed to be strikingly different from this.

The degree of psychological tension and conflict between the two parties was rather high. The city felt that it had taken the initiative by approaching the county for the purpose of resolving what the city saw as an almost desperate tax base crisis. Moreover, the city's initial policy was to pursue a program of revenue sharing, which was much more acceptable to the county than annexation. However, unbeknownst to the county, the city had also set a policy of negotiating for revenue sharing for a period of six months. The policy specified that if no agreement had been reached within that time period, the city would begin an annexation proceeding.

When this policy of a negotiation deadline was revealed during the course of the negotiations, the county became extremely upset. The county perceived the hidden deadline as an indication of dishonest intentions on the part of the city—the city's true intent was to seek annexation. The county also believed that the delayed revelation of the deadline was a calculated, high-handed attempt to exert pressure on the county to compromise quickly on revenue sharing. After seeing the county's reaction, the city said it understood the county's viewpoint and sought to conciliate. The city lifted its deadline as a gesture in this direction. It was shortly after this meeting that the county filed its immunity petition.

At this point both sides felt deceived and sold out. The county felt this way because of the secret deadline. The city believed the county's petitioning for immunity so shortly after the city's attempt at conciliation indicated that the county had been preparing its immunity action all along. Neither saw the other party as having negotiated in good faith.

When talks resumed after the commission's report on Oceanside's immunity petition was made public, both sides saw themselves in a somewhat advantaged position. The commission had denied Oceanside's request for immunity. The city felt the commission's action implied that the commission would favorably regard a case for annexation. (The city believed that the county must acknowledge this conclusion.) The county, on the other hand, noted that the commission's vote on immunity was not clear-cut, leaving open the possibility that after some delay the commission would favor the county. The county believed it had leverage in Richmond and state politics generally, so that political maneuvering was a viable tactic. As a result of these perceptions, the first meeting of the parties after the announcement of the commission's immunity report was marked by strong emotion and a general air of high conflict. A compensatory pattern developed in the following meetings: The meetings became "love feasts" (in the words of the participants), events wth little engagement of substantive issues.

Both parties felt that they had a stake in presenting an image of reasonable cooperativeness to the public because the main thrust of the commission's policy was to have parties settle disputes through mediated negotiation. Hence, if the conflict went before the commission for decision and the commission concluded that a party had made a sincere, good-faith attempt to negotiate the conflict, then this party's position would be enhanced. Moreover, if the negotiations appeared to fail because the other party was unreasonable, had negotiated in bad faith, or was recalcitrant, the commission would be more likely to look with favor on one's own petition. Despite the mediators' claims to the contrary, each party more than once indicated it thought that part of the mediators' role was to report to the commission on the reasonableness of the parties' behavior in the negotiations. Although this factor created a certain air of suspicion about the mediators, it nonetheless had a net positive effect in regulating the behavior of the parties within lines that were conducive to the continuation of the negotiations.

Other observations by the mediators on the background situation bear noting. The county had determined that a substantial problem it faced in dealing with the city was that the city's negotiating team was taking a less conciliatory stance toward the county than the whole council would have taken had it been the negotiating party and that this posture of the city negotiators was not fully communicated to the council. The county group found it difficult to understand the motives behind the mayor's behavior. Thus, they assumed that he was not acting in good faith. The undisclosed deadline mentioned earlier heavily conditioned this attitude.

Another factor affecting the county's stance in the proceedings was its feeling that the amount of land Virginia City had in mind to annex (a total of eighteen square miles) was so excessive that the city's case would fail decisively before the commission. The county anticipated that the commission would rebuke the city for such an excessive request in its report on the city's proposed annexation and, consequently, that the city would adopt a different negotiating posture. This viewpoint, of course, gave the county an incentive to delay or protract the negotiations until the commission's hearings and report.

In their initial meeting with the city negotiating team and the city council, the mediators explored the question of what role they would play in the negotiations. The city and the county initially believed that mediators put pressure on parties to induce compromise, which led to the parties' apprehension that if either side seemed more appealing to the mediators, the mediators might apply pressure unfairly. In response to this concern, the mediators explained that they, like the other parties to the negotiations, would act as representatives of a set of interests— the interests of the process of negotiation. The only pressure that they would apply would be to keep the process going. For an agreement to be successful, all parties must wholly and willingly accede to it. Hence, the mediators said, putting pressure on the parties for the sake of agreement alone would be counterproductive to the true purposes of both the negotiations and the mediators' own aims. The terms of resolution of the issues between the two parties had to be created by the parties themselves so that they could own the agreement. Although the city team acknowledged the reasonableness of this view, both it and the county team at various points in the negotiations wondered out loud whether the mediators were disregarding higher concerns to act in the interests of their own professional stakes—to be successful in gaining an agreement, *any* agreement.

Another area that the city wished to explore (as did the county side later) was the extent to which the mediators could reveal to one side information they gained in caucus sessions with the other side. The mediators quickly and strongly affirmed that all information from caucuses would be held in the strictest confidence. One member of the city team asked: "but can you tell us whether they are really serious about the negotiations and negotiating in good faith so that we will know when and if we are just wasting our time?" The mediators replied that they wanted to make a clear stipulation to both sides: if at any point the mediators felt that one or both sides were not negotiating in good faith, they would exit themselves from the process. And the mediators told both sides, "as long as we are involved in the talks, you will have evidence that in our best judgment both sides are negotiating in good faith." (In spite of the mediators' declaration about the confidentiality of the meetings with them, on numerous occasions one or the other party would ask them to leave caucus sessions while strategy was being formulated. The lack of trust seemed to be a natural part of the negotiation proceedings.)

The mediators went on to explain that a key part of their role was to specify, represent, and seek to gain continuing compliance with a set of ground rules, or operating norms, for the negotiating teams. A list of ten such rules had been spelled out in a document that both sides had agreed to in a meeting in late September, 1984. These rules covered a wide range of basic format issues for the meetings, and in reviewing the list, the mediators noted that all of them were congruent with the mediators' own sense of a good negotiation process. In fact, a number of the rules—those specifying that the meetings be held in executive session, that all members of the teams were bound by a rule of confidentiality, that no proposals made in the negotiations could be used for any purpose in any administrative or judicial proceedings, and that only one joint statement to the press would be made at the conclusion of each meeting—duplicated specifications that the mediators wanted to make. The mediators suggested an addition to the list: that they be designated as the press representatives for the parties and that the press statement issued after each meeting should be a simple standardized notice stipulating that a meeting had been held and that further meetings were or were not scheduled. Such a standardized statement should be used at least until such time as there were substantive matters to make known to the public. This was readily agreed to by the parties.

The mediators described and explained a number of other norms of negotiation that they felt were essential for the parties to recognize and accept: (1) The negotiating teams should be able to make proposals, receive proposals, express agreement and disagreement, and otherwise react on the spot to the presentations made by the other team; (2) each side should explicitly acknowledge that it cannot compel the other side to agree to its proposals or even make the other side consider its proposals; (3) a side that received a proposal, even if it did not wish to consider it, had the responsibility to specify to the other side what was objectionable about the proposal and to respond by formulating and presenting an alternative proposal to the other side; and (4) the two teams should be balanced in representation of elected officials; that is, the number of elected officials on each side should be equal.

The mediators went on to indicate that their role would be to provide structure and some direction to the process by calling caucuses, requesting proposals, and so forth; however, they would maintain a low profile and would make the minimum interventions required in order to keep the negotiating process alive and well. Another part of their role, they noted, was to facilitate communication by helping the parties to express their perspectives clearly and to listen accurately to each other. They also said they would play a conflict resolution role by identifying patterns of conflict-evoking interactions and making the parties aware of these. The mediators asked the teams to identify the style of negotiating they wanted to employ. Styles include outright bargaining (back-and-forth bargaining), the style associated with horse trading, joint problem solving, or a learning process, whereby the two sides gather information and use it as a base for creating mutually acceptable answers to the issues. The city negotiators wanted to treat the negotiations like a business deal in which one asks a higher price than another is willing to accept or, alternatively, one offers a lower price than another is willing to pay, then both exchange offers until establishing a price acceptable to both. The mediators acceded to this view at that point because the county side expressed the same perspective and because the parties should choose the style of negotiating. The negotiators indicated that such a negotiating posture was a good place from which to begin, then added that in other cases that had been settled successfully, the settlement came when the parties identified their vital interests clearly, moved away from specific bargaining-type issues (for example, where the annexation line should be drawn), to consideration of other matters that broadened their perspective on the situation, and problem solved collaboratively from this broader perspective. The mediators acknowledged that this style of negotiating probably did not make much sense to the parties at this point in the negotiation and that the mediators expected an eventual change to it if the parties' selected bargaining style did not lead to a settlement.

Discussions of ground rules and other preliminary matters were conducted with the county also. Then discussion turned to the substance of the negotiations themselves. The city expressed that it could not understand why the county was being as negative as it had been in the negotiations. To the city, the county appeared as wanting to focus the talks on the option of revenue sharing. The city believed it had shown clear willingness to consider this option from the start of the controversy. The real picture, as the city saw it at that point, was that the county wanted no change at all—that is, the county did not want revenue sharing, but revenue sharing was better than annexation.

At this point the mediators proposed a refocusing of the talks within a different framework. In their view, the talks had come to a difficult pass because the parties had begun the negotiations from a perspective so broad (economic growth and revenue sharing) that they could not identify their vital interests. The mediators felt that only when they identified these interests to some extent would movement in the talks begin to occur within the framework of their broad perspective. This was the pattern of negotiation that they had observed in other cases—namely, that as parties began to specify their bottom-line interests and to make these known, communications improved and a negotiating environment that could lead to agreement prevailed. Paradoxically tensions often rise while the communications and negotiating environment improve. Therefore, the mediators suggested that the parties stop talking about the broad topic of revenue sharing and instead begin considering specifically where a mutually acceptable annexation line could be drawn.

This proposal was received with ambivalence by the city group. The city manager and one or two others voiced the opinion that talking about annexation was probably the simplest and clearest way to address the general issue of Virginia City's situation. Others were concerned that the county team, given their extremely strong reactions to any mention of annexation in past meetings, would flatly reject this approach. They were also concerned that the rapport between the two teams would be damaged further because the county team would suspect that the initiative for focusing discussion on annexation had come from the city side. Some members of the city council stated that the voters of Virginia City were more interested in revenue sharing than in annexation and that resistance could come from the voters. The mediators pointed out that, since the substance of the talks would not be made known to the public, it was not likely that this would be problem. The discussions ended on a rather ambiguous note—the city wanted to wait and see what the county's reaction to this idea would be. The mediators requested that the city prepare a proposal for presentation to the county at a joint meeting on May 7.

In their initial meeting with the county team, the mediators presented their idea of focusing the talks directly on the topic of where to draw an annexation line. This proposal was met with silence and then dismay. As the city had predicted, some members thought the mediators' proposal resulted from the mediators' closed talks just concluded with the city, proving that the city was really only interested in discussing annexation. The mediators explained that it was they who were making this suggestion, then outlined again the reasons for it. Most of the county group, however, remained unconvinced by the mediators' line of reasoning.

Phase 2: Formal Proposals

At the joint meeting on May 7, the first with the mediators present, the city initiated the talks with presentation of a proposal in written form. The proposal followed the general outlines of prior proposals that the city had made in talks before the mediators entered the case. It called for development of a joint revenue sharing program by which the city would receive funds from county real property and sales taxes.

The county viewed this proposal as a demand that it provide an unreasonable proportion of its tax revenue to the city. Furthermore, the plan would prevent the annexation of the land the city sought only for fifteen years. After that period revenue-sharing would expire and the city could petition to annex the land.

There was one point in the proposal that became the focus of the discussion at the meeting: the stipulation that there should be a back up provision to take effect if the revenue sharing effort failed (it would fail if the voters rejected it). A map was attached to the proposal, illustrating an automatic back-up annexation. The county team felt that the city was making a land grab under a rather flimsy pretense at revenue sharing and that their plan made it even easier to annex in the future than under current legal arrangements, affording the county even less security for its future development than it now had.

The saving grace of the proposal from the county's point of view was that the area designated on the map as the back-up annexation area was something less than the eighteen miles the city had formerly requested. Even so, the county felt insulted by the proposal. The county charged that the city was only interested in annexation and was not sincerely discussing revenue sharing. This was an emotional accusation, and little of substance was brought out. The mediators felt that a certain amount of venting was appropriate for both sides.

Five days later one of the mediators met with the two teams. This meeting was difficult and unproductive because the stalemate that had been building at the end of the prior meeting had now become fully developed. Because the county had received the last proposal, the city believed that it was the county's turn to submit a proposal. The county felt that the city had not made a sincere proposal and so no response was required; the county told the mediator to convey to the city that they would respond only after receiving another, serious proposal.

This incident was characteristic of this phase of the negotiations, and therefore warrants some discussion. The most persistent difficulty in this stage of the talks was that each side, a number of times, regarded an offer made to it as an affront, therefore refused to make a counter offer, then demanded another offer from the proposing side before responding. A number of factors were at work here. Because each side felt it had been deceived by the other, and because each had agreed to bring in mediators because they wanted the negotiations to move ahead, each side expected the other to offer a significant concession on the annexation line as a token of good faith negotiating and intentions of conciliation. When such concessions were not forthcoming, each side felt that the other was not acting in good faith.

Complicating this matter was the way in which the sides presented their proposals to each other. When in caucus with the mediators, each side frequently formulated proposals that were deemed as simply places to start talking from; they wanted to present the proposal only in order to get a reaction from the other side. When a party was planning to begin a meeting with this type of presentation, the mediators sometimes coached the presenters on how to discuss the proposal in a way that would evoke a response from the other side. Basically, their advice was to give a low key presentation and show interest in hearing the other side's reactions. Both parties rejected the advice and insisted on presenting every proposal, no matter how tentative or exploratory it might be, as their absolute bottom line position, a position from which there could be no retreat that represented painful and extreme concessions on their part. Naturally, given this sort of presentation, the receiving side would be likely to assume that the presenters were dead serious and see them as unreasonable. The receiving side would then become outraged and refuse to respond until another more sensible, good-faith offer had been put forth.

When the mediators reminded the participants of the agreed upon negotiating principle of responding even to proposals that one did not wish to consider seriously, the parties frequently retorted that to trade back and forth repeatedly—which is what they felt they would have to do in order to get to a reasonable middle ground—would mean they would have to act like horse traders rather than reasonable governmental leaders. It was only by appealing to the parties' self-concept as reasonable statesmen that the mediators were able to untangle this type of snarl.

In response to the city's joint revenue sharing proposal, the county asked the city what it was willing to give in return for any possible concession from the county. This was an oblique bid to discuss permanent immunity from annexation for the county. The city's response was that it had already made a concession on the back up line—this was what it was giving up. The county replied that the city was trading with something that it did not have in the first place—namely, the land concessions—since these were presently in the county. After some discussion on this point the talks ended.

One week later both mediators met with the two negotiating teams in their separate caucuses. It became clear in these discussions that the county saw the city as unwilling to negotiate seriously. What had to happen, in the county's view, was that the city must be made to realize that its demand for an eighteen-square mile annexation was "ridiculous." The county also felt that the city would lessen its annexation demands only when the commission issued its report on their annexation request. Seeing the situation in this way disposed the county to play a waiting game, simply protracting the talks until the report came out months later. The mediators counseled that the situation might change for the worse after the hearings because the substantial cost of the hearings to the city might dispose it to annexation to recoup spent funds. The county was not swayed by this caution.

After this meeting the mediators discussed the county's strategy. They concluded that given this strategy, the county could not maintain a good-faith stance. The mediators then drafted the following press release:

> The state-appointed mediators in the Virginia City/Oceanside County annexation/immunity negotiations today recommended to the negotiating teams a suspension of formal negotiations to a date following the issuance of the report by the Commission on Local Government on Virginia City's annexation petition. While the talks between the two negotiating teams have developed a useful dialogue on the issues of governmental consolidation and annexation, the mediators see the list of questions involved as so lengthy and complex that they would benefit from clarification by the Commission on Local Government's hearings and their subsequent report.

They then took the press release to the offices of both the city manager and the county administrator to get their reactions to it before releasing it to the public. Within the next two hours, each official called the mediators at their hotel and expressed rather urgent concern that the talks continue. They reported that they were speaking for their governing boards.

In assessing this turn of events, the mediators speculated that each side either saw itself as not negotiating in good faith or feared that the mediators held this opinion. Perhaps, the mediators thought, both sides feared that if the commission suspected that a party had not negotiated in good faith, the commission would be biased against that side's case in any subsequent commission proceedings.

The talks resumed one week later with one mediator present. The climate of the situation had changed markedly. The city presented a new and more conciliatory line for the back-up annexation area. The county responded positively and made a number of gestures of approval toward the city's new stance.

The city's proposal was presented to the county board a few days later. The board believed the proposal was not deserving of a conciliatory response. The board drafted a counterproposal with a completely county-oriented line. The city responded to the county proposal with dismay and even an open show of disgust. The county caucused after that meeting; they worked late into the night and developed some concessions on a new line. At the next meeting the city strongly rejected this new line.

In caucus, after much internal team conciliation work, the city agreed upon yet another new line that it felt reflected the positive discussions and signals of agreement it had seen when it first presented a changed stance on the back-up annexation area. The county rejected this proposal too. The mediators then suggested various compromises that might be considered, but no new line of discussion emerged. The meeting adjourned after agreement had been reached to continue the talks with at least one subsequent meeting.

The sort of back-and-forth exchange just described is characteristic of talks during this stage of positional bargaining. Each side was attempting to move the other into a compromised position by the strength of rejection of the proposal put forth. At various points, such tactics did work successfully in evoking concessions and a change toward a more conciliatory attitude on the other side, but none of the concessions brought about in this manner were sufficient to satisfy either side that the talks were progressing. The focus of attention was almost totally on the question of where to draw the so-called back-up annexation line, that is, the line that demarked the area of a friendly annexation if the revenue-sharing plan failed. The county believed that its vital interest in pursuing the feasibility of revenue-sharing was ignored by the city in the discussions. The city, on the other hand, felt that the county was refusing to recognize that revenue sharing was a valid option the city wished to consider. Both sides were looking for a significant concrete concession on the annexation line as a demonstration of good faith, and both remained disappointed.

Outside of the talks, certain exogenous factors were working to contribute to these difficulties. The county team members were convinced that the city's negotiating team was the problem; they felt that the council as a whole favored revenue sharing over annexation. Citizen opinion in the city, as the county saw it, favored revenue sharing rather heavily. There was much public criticism about the costs of the annexation proceedings. The county developed a strategy based on these points: (1) to make representations through the press that Virginia City could not afford the annexation (that is, neither the costs of the suit nor the payback costs to the county) and (2) to call for joint negotiating sessions between the city council and the county board. The county also suggested that joint public meetings be held just to air the issues and provide public information. There was some evidence that the county side was correct in its assessment of the need to air the issues: some of the council seemed puzzled in caucus sessions about why there appeared to be so much difficulty in the negotiations. It had been approved that any member of the city council or city board could attend the negotiating sessions as silent observers. However, this allowance had little or no impact on the proceedings.

This stage of the talks did serve a number of positive purposes, however. First, it allowed the mediators to see the two sides encounter each other under conditions of conflict and near stalemate. As a result the mediators could diagnose any process-related issues that were contributing to the problems the parties were having with each other. These were primarily communication issues, and the mediators worked on them with the teams individually and by making process interventions during the talks. Therefore this stage helped the teams to learn how to talk with each other.

Second, although there was great frustration surrounding the exchange of proposals about the back-up annexation line, this process did produce some substantive movement in the positions of the two parties. The slow and difficult process of reformulating positions in response to each other did lay an important foundation for the processes that would characterize the next stage of the negotiations.

Most important, however, was that during this phase the mediators were able to work with the city team on the critical matter of developing an image of what the county's vital interests were. The mediators had, from their involvement in the county's caucuses, a fairly good sense of how the county saw its vital interests. Indeed, in discussions with the county's special attorney, the mediators had learned of some of the county's concerns about the city's annexation. As pointed out earlier, one of the county's main interests was to secure a place with permanent immunity from annexation where it could develop a type of county seat office complex. It also had an interest in protecting some of its developed areas from annexation through permanent immunity.

The mediators, however, in keeping with their agreement with both sides, could not in any way make this information known to the city negotiators. Over the course of the weeks of positional bargaining, though, whenever the city team itself moved toward a proposal that acknowledged these interests of the county, the mediators could reinforce and validate such discussions with comments like, "That looks like an interesting proposal to us; why don't we see what the county thinks of it." Through this process the city team did come to understand, at least in part, what the main vital interests of the county were.

Our description of the negotiations resumes with the events immediately following the apparent stalemate on where to draw the back-up annexation line. The county moved to soften and broaden the negotiations by proposing, at a meeting on June 17, that the two parties appoint a committee to study the feasibility and desirability of developing a joint revenue sharing plan.

As part of this proposal, the county called for suspension of all annexation and immunity hearings. The city responded that even though it was amenable to the idea of a study of revenue sharing—indeed it seemed essential that such a study be carried out before revenue sharing would be possible—it could not agree to stop pursuing its annexation case in a timely manner. The reason for this, the city noted, was that it could not afford to let the data base for its annexation case get out of date; if the annexation case was resumed much later, the city would be compelled to hire expensive consultants to update the data. The county probably interpreted this response as evidence of bad faith negotiating and a run-around. The characteristic of bad faith negotiating was confirmed for the county when on June 24 the local paper carried a story about a public briefing on annexation that the city was holding. In a city handbook prepared for that meeting and subsequent public distribution, both annexation and revenue sharing were discussed, but strong emphasis was placed on the point that the annexation proceedings could not be delayed. Also, the county considered some of the language in the pamphlet biased and polemical. The county's reaction was close to outrage. The talks were again at a very difficult pass.

Phase 3: Collaborative Problem Solving

It was at this rather inauspicious point, however, that the negotiations began to move into the problem-solving mode. Collaborative problem solving is a stage marked by a degree of mutual trust, acknowledgment of the vital interests of the other side, rather high efficiency of communication, and creative efforts to design alternatives. How was the transition made to this most positive of all negotiation modes?

Step one occurred when the mediators next met with the teams in caucuses. The county team members at that point had virtually lost all confidence that the city was seriously interested in joint revenue sharing—they thought the city wanted only annexation. The city, ironically, no longer believed that the county would consider revenue sharing—they thought the county wanted only to delay and deny any sort of change at all. The mediators presented themselves as the parties largely responsible for the confusion. They told the two teams that they had perhaps contributed to some of the difficulty in the talks by pressing the parties to focus on where to draw an annexation line rather than on the broader question of revenue sharing.

The mediators assured the city team that it was their sincere belief that the county would pursue a revenue sharing agreement in good faith. When the mediators met with the county team, they were met with the outcry: "We have never even really heard the word revenue sharing from the city—can you tell us they are even interested in it, much less serious about it!" The mediators responded by saying that the emphasis on annexation came from themselves, that it was at their request that the talks had focused so much on the annexation line, and that the city was truly interested in studying the possibility of joint revenue sharing. They pointed out that at this highly preliminary stage neither the county nor the city could declare unequivocally that they were in favor of revenue sharing; revenue sharing was highly complex and would have to be studied carefully before anyone would know the full consequences of it. The county agreed with this observation and went on to say that what they were looking for was some evidence that the city was considering anything besides trying to take county land. The mediators stressed repeatedly that in their view the city had honest intentions to consider other options.

Step two in the transition to the problem-solving stage came with the city's realization and acknowledgment of the county's vital interests in permanent immunity from annexation for certain areas of the county. It was this concrete acknowledgment by the city that made the mediators' words to the county about the city's motives seem real, even though talk about where to draw a possible annexation line of course continued. It was when the city showed willingness to agree to permanent immunity that the major affective dimension of the county's vital interests was revealed. It was in the context of discussing the need for permanent immunity that with some poignancy the county spoke of feeling like beleaguered Indians who faced an incessant threat of having their land taken away and who had no secure place where they could build a home and a way of life. It was this somewhat defensive feeling that had been giving so much energy to the protests of the county to the talk of annexation and, perhaps, what made it difficult for the county to be explicit about what it wanted in the way of immunity because the county would have revealed its most vital interest.

The duration of the problem-solving stage in this case was rather brief probably because (1) the level of interpersonal tension between the two sides was considerably more than minimal, (2) their interests were rather congruent on the key matter of revenue sharing (and probably had been from the start of the dispute), and (3) the various pieces of a possible agreement had already been worked out—namely, the idea of agreeing to a study of revenue sharing, the notion of a back-up annexation line and where it could be drawn, and the acknowledgment of the county's interest in permanent immunity. What was needed in the way of problem solving was for each side to trust that the other was sincerely interested in proceeding with work on revenue sharing in a timely manner, which was one of the vital interests of the city.

Problem solving around this issue was one of the two main break-throughs of the negotiations. The problem that was blocking the parties from agreeing to the concept of studying revenue sharing was that even were a revenue sharing plan to be worked out and put before the voters, the county felt the city could either openly or surreptitiously work against the proposal and have it voted down, leaving the city with a low-cost, problem-free automatic annexation of the area designated by the back-up line. The county thus supposed that the city could be simply pursuing annexation by a circuitous route.

The city had similar suspicions about the county. The city perceived any type of delay as in the county's interest because it had been generally acknowledged in Virginia that superior finances and protracted delays through the courts were the two main advantages that counties have in annexation cases. A revenue sharing study would allow the county an additional possibility for delay through the courts. One strategy the county could pursue would be to carry out the revenue sharing study, then work against approval of the plan by county voters. The city would then be left to face a year-long, enormously expensive court battle in addition to having to pay the cost of hiring consultants to update the data base necessary to pursue the annexation battle before the commission and in court.

The scheme that was devised for working around this problem was developed in a series of meetings in late June and early July. The basic concept came from the city side, specifically from the mayor and the city manager. What the city proposed was a contingency approach to revenue sharing that would, first, involve both sides in designing and funding a study of how to construct a joint revenue sharing program— an idea that had been considered in the negotiations from their beginnings. Then, assuming that a satisfactory revenue sharing plan could be worked out with the help of consultants, the plan would be put before the voters of the county and the city, as required by law. If both the city and county voters approved the plan, a joint revenue sharing program would be established. If, on the other hand, the city voters approved revenue sharing and the county voters rejected it, the contingency plan was to grant the city a friendly automatic annexation by the county of a larger area than the city would have accepted in a negotiated settlement. In another scenario in which city voters rejected revenue sharing and county voters approved it, the city would be granted a friendly annexation, but of an area smaller in size than it would have accepted in a negotiated settlement and one that excluded certain areas the city considered important to have. If both sets of voters rejected the revenue sharing plan, a friendly annexation would occur wherein the city would be granted an annexation area that would be less than it would have received under the first contingency plan that was described, but more than it would have gotten if only the city voters had rejected the plan.

This concept of multiple alternatives came from the mayor in response to a deadlock over a specific land area the city and the county were contending about. Under all of these contingencies the county was to receive permanent immunity for the area it wanted to protect from annexation. In effect then, this scheme gave each side an incentive to pursue the revenue sharing plan sincerely. A win-win strategy had been found.

When this concept, called a double-back-up line, was introduced, a new air settled over the talks, at least for a while. The positive attitude with which this idea was greeted by both sides derived from an underlying acknowledgment by the parties that it did seem, after all, that the other side was willing to consider seriously the prospect of revenue sharing. There was then a moment of good feeling and mutual good will; however, this feeling was not celebrated or made manifest in any overt way. Expression of it was subdued; the tone was like the sigh of relief expected from parties recognizing that at last they were going to be taken seriously.

The problem-solving phase for this case was so short that it was more like a rite of passage than like a phase. The development of and agreement upon the double-back-up line allowed movement beyond the negative feelings of the competitive bargaining stage. The scheme itself, however, was too mechanical and simple to have required the collaborative effort necessary for a true rapport to develop and for the competitive and mistrustful feelings that the parties held to be worked through in any lasting way. As a consequence, the proceedings rather quickly reverted to another round of competitive bargaining.

Phase 4: Return to Competitive Bargaining

The focus of the renewed competitive bargaining was the issue of where to draw the various back-up annexation lines called for by the scheme. Attention focused on two areas: a section along a major highway to the east of the current boundary of the city (eastern area) and an area to the west of the city (western area). In particular for these two areas, the issues concerned the location of the boundaries of the immunity area.

The bargaining over these matters was very much like the earlier competitive jockeying for positions. In this instance, however, the talks became even more difficult because much of the time attention focused on the eastern area, about which feelings were especially high on the part of both parties.

Two factors affected the county's feelings over the eastern area. One factor was the county's belief that there was historical documentation that the city in the past had explicitly and emphatically rejected the possibility of taking the eastern area within its boundary. There seemed to be a feeling that this area was a kind of orphan that for some reason (perhaps relating to the rural identification of the people and businesses in the eastern area) the city had cast out and the county had taken under its wing. The city team vehemently denied this account of the history of the area. The other factor influencing the county's position over the area was that one of the members of the county negotiating team directly represented it, and he carried with him a strong opinion that the people in that area were against its becoming part of the city. To lose the eastern area to the city would mean, it seemed, certain loss of his seat on the county board of supervisors.

From the city's point of view, the eastern area was perhaps the most natural or reasonable place to be annexed. The city denied it had ever rejected taking in this area and expressed that the area was a virtual part of the city: "Just drive out there and look for yourself," the city negotiating team told the mediators, "the area is adjacent to the city and you can't tell where the city ends and the eastern area begins. The eastern area is the city." Not to bring this area within the city's borders therefore made no sense to the city, if for no other reason than the aesthetics of drawing the annexation line. It would, they felt, be absurd to leave this area out of the annexation.

As a result of these two opposing views, competitive bargaining became quite intense. The mediators at several points suggested trade offs from other sections of the map to gain a compromised line for the eastern area. Interspersed throughout these sessions were regular intense outbursts over an essentially semantic issue about the city's guarantee of immunity to the county. In the discussions the city employed the term "immunity" to refer to the western area. When the county heard this term it was usual for hands to slap down on the table top and for one of the county team to cry out something like: "Immunity! What do you mean, immunity?! We are talking about permanent, in perpetuity immunity! So why can't you, or won't you say that?" This linguistic habit of the city's so irritated the county that it caused a more perceptible air of distrust to creep into the talks. The county's interpretation of the use of the term was that it was an unconscious signal that the city was not serious about its offer of permanent immunity. Hence, the mediators simply began insisting on the phrase "permanent immunity" every time the city referred to this matter.

What finally resolved the issue of the eastern area is that the discussions over a double-back-up annexation line allowed space for each side to make the sort of declaration of emotion that it wanted to make to the other side. If the county voters rejected revenue sharing, the annexation line would include all of the eastern area. The city declared regarding this outcome: "This is the line from which we will not retreat!" In drawing the annexation line that would take effect if county voters approved revenue sharing but city voters rejected it, the county team made the same emphatic declaration—their line allowed all of the eastern area to remain in the county. Agreement on the third line—the compromise annexation that would take effect if both parties rejected the revenue sharing plan (and hence neither were to be rewarded with the eastern area)—became essentially a technical task of splitting the difference between the land marked out by the other two lines, which was accomplished by a consultation between the county administrator and the city manager.

Consensus on the general scheme was worked out at a lengthy meeting of the entire city and county governing boards at the county office building on Friday, July 18. What remained at that point was the redrafting of a final document that would sharply focus the remaining detailed issues needing to be addressed in an agreement. This document was the vehicle that carried the talks into the final, agreement stage.

Phase 5: The Agreement Stage

What distinguishes the agreement stage of negotiations is that the talks in the stage proceed under a constitutional umbrella, even though positional bargaining and some contentiousness continue and significant specific issues still remain to be addressed. In the agreement stage both parties see themselves as standing on the common ground of a general consensus they have reached on an outline of an agreement. The document that had been prepared for consideration at the July 18 meeting served as the working symbol of this general consensus. The core of it, the double-back-up line plan, was agreed to by the full governing boards of both sides. Therefore, the document carried with it something of the air of a constitution on which attention was focused for the purpose of considering amendments.

Due to a scheduling conflict, only one of the mediators was able to attend the meetings scheduled for July 21. The mediator's first caucus was with the city, to consider the document that had emerged from the July 18 meeting. This document called for the city and the county to collaborate in having a study carried out to "produce a single plan for the sharing of certain revenues of the two governments."

In its detailed consideration of the document, two major issues arose from the city side. The first of these concerned a provision of the document that stipulated only that the "joint revenue sharing was to be binding on the communities." In a later version, drawn by the county, a sentence was added specifying that the revenue sharing agreement "may be renegotiated at the request of either party" ten years after commencement of the plan. The wording of this provision caused the city great concern because the word "may" seemed to leave open the possibility that the city might be locked into a revenue sharing formula that did not cover important potential county revenue sources. Various alternative wordings were considered, with choices ultimately being narrowed simply to changing the word "may" to "can," "shall," or "will." Consensus formed finally on substituting "will" for "may."

Another provision of the document received the most attention; several hours were spent discussing it. This provision concerned the effect of outside decisionmakers—the courts—on the negotiated settlement. The provision stated that if the court reviewing the revenue sharing plan altered the terms of it, then either party could abandon the revenue sharing plan. A further statement in this provision indicated that if the court required changes in the original agreement, the parties would make an effort to renegotiate a settlement acceptable to the court.

The effect of this provision was to make the entire workability of the plan contingent on trustworthiness of the two sides to make a diligent effort to renegotiate a new agreement if the court modified the original agreement. It was at this point that the brevity of the problem-solving stage of the negotiations and the mechanical nature of the consensus that underpinned the talks thus far became evident. Although the city seemed motivated to move toward settlement, it simply did not trust an agreement that gave the county the opportunity to delay progress toward solving the city's problems (the opportunity for delay was the time the study would take). Furthermore, the court-ordered changes provision provided the county an easy escape clause. The city still did not believe that the county sincerely wanted to consider revenue sharing or any sort of change. The city attorney, in particular, urged his clients to take a cautious and conservative stance.

The mediator's approach to what appeared to be a certain foundering of the agreement was both practical and conceptual. On the practical side, he noted that it was a "the Gods are laughing" situation that both parties from the beginning of the talks had listed revenue sharing as their first line of consideration for approaching the dispute and yet, after months of hard, sometimes agonizing work, neither side believed that the other wanted it. He reiterated that in the view of both mediators, revenue sharing was seriously a possibility, depending on the outcome of a detailed study of it. He noted that the county side spoke of the city in the same terms that the city was now using about the county. In spite of giving this line of argument a rather impassioned tone, it seemed fairly clear from the nonverbal reactions around the table that it had little convincing effect. The mediator next mentioned the costs of the negotiations thus far and stated that an agreement that might avoid further costs inherent in the hearing process that was about to begin was possibly within an inch of being grasped. This point seemed to be received rather well.

The conceptual part of the mediators' approach concerned the possibility of completely revising the offending section using new legislation just then emerging from the state legislature.[5] This proposed legislation, as will be detailed shortly, provided that voluntary agreements reached between local governments be given a special status before the Commission on Local Government and the courts that would make them, in effect, binding in their own right. He went on to say that this matter would need to be examined further. He suggested that since the meeting had gone on for hours and the caucus session with the county was to meet soon, he could carry the city's amended version of the document to the county caucus, discuss the issue of the proposed legislation with them, and discuss with the county and the city attorneys the feasibility of applying the legislation to this situation. The mediator agreed with the city team that it and its governing board would be ready to meet later that night if it seemed that applying the legislation was either necessary or possibly productive.

At the county caucus that evening, the initial atmosphere was rather tense and mixed with positive and negative overtones. On the positive side, an agreement was definitely afoot; three lines of negative sentiment were also active. One of these was a sense that the county had conceded too much on the back-up annexation lines and that possibly these lines should be redrawn, especially in the eastern area. Second was the sense that the county was trading away something for nothing. Recent articles in the Richmond newspaper had suggested that the idea of permanent immunity might not be recognized by the courts on the grounds that a present governing body could not tie the hands of future governing bodies to act in response to their constituents' wishes. (This concern was voiced vigorously by the member of the county's negotiating team who represented the eastern area.) Third, the county had the same sorts of concern about the provision concerning court-ordered changes that the city had—that it would afford the city an easy escape clause. The county felt they would probably use it because they were "not serious about pursuing revenue-sharing anyway." The concern about the court's possibly denying permanent immunity intensified the concern about the provision's being an escape clause, since if the court did deny permanent immunity, it would amount to the substantial modification needed in order for the escape clause to be activated.

The mediator remained quiet while these negative concerns were given a full airing. Then he intervened to note that, first, he strongly urged against any reconsideration of the lines as these had been agreed to by both governing boards after lengthy discussion. He reminded the county of the advantages of a settlement at this point and stated that he felt a settlement was definitely at hand. Second, he brought up the new legislation, explained it, and indicated in the process how it might provide a definite way of meeting the county's concerns about ensuring permanent immunity and obviating the escape clause.

Before this county caucus session, the mediator had met with the county attorney and discussed the new legislation. By happenstance, the city attorney had dropped by the county office building during their meeting so he also joined the discussion. They looked up the proposed legislation in the county manager's legislative proceedings book and the county attorney briefly studied its specific wording. The proposed bill provided that if local jurisdictions could reach voluntary settlement of annexation, transition, revenue sharing, or immunity issues, they could modify or waive, in whole or in part, certain requirements theretofore provided by the Virginia Code. This provision gave broadened scope and flexibility to the negotiation process. Agreements were to then be submitted to the Commission on Local Government for an advisory review and then sent on to circuit court for an order establishing the agreement. However, the statute limited the court review in such a way as to make the proceeding favor the agreement. A last important point is that the statute explicitly stated that the agreements would be binding on future governing bodies.

The mediator mentioned the legislation in the meeting of the county board and asked the county attorney to comment. The attorney affirmed to the county board that the legislation did seem to make it possible for the county and the city to make a binding agreement to permanent immunity. The board listened with obvious interest. The mood of the group seemed to become quite positive as they sensed the possibility of a breakthrough to an agreement. They asked the mediator whether the proposal had become law. The mediator responded that he was relatively certain that it had become, or was about to become law; he offered to get confirmation. They unanimously urged him to get definite word about the status of the legislation as soon as possible. That was at about 9:00 P.M.

The mediator left the room and began placing telephone calls around the state in an attempt to determine the status of the legislative proposal. After calling his colleague, members of the Commission on Local Government staff, and various officials around the state, he was able to discover that the legislation had passed both houses in the General Assembly and that the governor had scheduled a date for the signing ceremony. The mediator returned to the meeting and reported what he had learned. The fact that the proposal was not yet law gave the board pause, even though its signing by the governor, which seemed imminent, was all that remained to be done to make it a law. After discussions of about twenty minutes, the county board decided to proceed as though the proposal was law; the board directed the county attorney to incorporate it in the agreement by rewriting the relevant provision of the agreement.

Then the mediator turned attention to another important topic: the question of how to ensure that the city would have an absolute right to renegotiate the revenue sharing package if, after a period of time, it felt it was not getting a fair share of city-county revenues. The reader will recall that this issue focused specifically on one word of one sentence in the provision describing the revenue sharing concept. The sentence read: "Ten years from the commencement of this agreement the revenue sharing agreement *may* (emphasis added) be renegotiated at the request of either of the parties." The contested word was "may." The city wanted to change "may" to "must," thereby ensuring, in its view, that the revenue sharing study could not result in a plan that left the city tied to a static revenue formula while the county's revenue base was expanding.

Raising this issue chilled the air. Tempers began to rise as the county group discussed the city's demand. On the one hand, they saw the change as an incidental, unimportant detail. On the other hand, they saw it as a rather pointed insult to the county, which was the catalyst to the change in climate of the meeting. The feeling of insult derived from the county's perception that it had never done anything in the negotiations to indicate that it had any interest in using revenue sharing as a way of undercutting the city. It surely had never been raised as an issue until this late point. Furthermore, coming from the city as it did, the county felt it indicated suspicion and ill will of one set of elected officials toward another. The main point of the county's discussion was that contesting the word was a nonissue and therefore the city was wrong to have tried to make it an issue. The county, therefore, refused to make the change, saying that "the city is going to have to show a little trust."

Discussion turned to the question of how the proposal should be presented to the city. It was quickly determined that the mediator should take the county's proposal to the city (just as he had brought the city's proposal to the county).

The last matter taken up by the board was how the agreement, if it occurred, should be announced. They moved into a mode of intensive strategy formulation about how they could employ the settlement to their best advantage before the State Commission on Local Government. The plan they devised was highly dramatic. They decided to demand that the city agree to hold a joint press conference just before the commission hearings were to begin, in front of the building where the hearings were to take place. Thus, as the public, the local government officials and their attorneys, and the commission members filed into the building where the county was to fight it out, they would directly witness a celebration of a voluntary settlement that the county had reached with the city. Perhaps the press would even interview some of the commission members about their reaction to the settlement—reactions that of course would be highly positive toward both the city and the county.

As a last point, the county asked the mediator whether in his view the city would accept the proposal as the county had revised it. The mediator responded that he thought that the escape clause provision would probably be accepted, but that perhaps the county had underestimated the intensity of the city's feelings about the "may" and "must" issue of the paragraph addressing the renegotiation of the revenue sharing plan. Having recalled that it was a similar attempt to manipulate the setting for the final settlement meeting in another dispute that had been partly instrumental in those talks breaking down, the mediator went on to say that they might have to reconsider how to announce any settlement that might occur. In response, the county pointed out that holding the press conference at the state library outside of the city where the commission hearings were to be held was putting it on neutral ground.

The meeting then adjourned. It was about 10:30 P.M. at that point. The county manager called in his secretary to retype the agreement. The mediator called the city aside, telling them that the county wished to make a counterproposal. The mediator added that he would like to meet with the entire city side (the negotiating team and the council) at midnight. As it turned out, the retyping of the revised proposal was not completed by midnight; hence, the mediator decided to proceed to the city's offices, begin the discussions, and have the revised proposals brought over later.

When the city convened at midnight, the climate in the room was charged but ambivalent. The sense of anticipation that a settlement was imminent was strong, but there was also a powerful tone of caution, set largely by the city attorney. When the mediator entered the room, he noted with surprised alarm that the city's special attorneys for the annexation suit were present. Although he thought they might be helpful to the talks at this stage, their presence alarmed him because the county had such strong feelings that these (outside lawyers) had been blocking the county from reaching a settlement.

After taking care to close the meeting room door, the mediator began the meeting by reporting that the revised proposals would be brought over later, after typing and copying were complete, and that he wished, given the late hour, to immediately begin the discussions. He then proceeded carefully through his own notated draft of the proposal and described the changes the county was proposing.

Attention focused on the only two problem areas the proposal seemed to contain: the ten-year renegotiation provision and the escape clause. A lengthy and intensive discussion ensued concerning the county board's resistance to changing the wording from "may" to "must." Serious concern was expressed, led by the city attorney, about signing an agreement with such disputed wording. Suspicions about the county began to arise: "Why wouldn't they make such a simple change? What are they up to?" The idea of compromising with the word "can" was considered but dropped because "can" did not provide the kind of insurance the city wanted. The mediator explained the county's view of the matter—that the city's raising this issue was simply a gesture of mistrust to which they did not want to respond.

At about 1:00 A.M., there was a knock on the closed door of the meeting room. The mediator went to the door, walked out into the hall, and closed the door firmly behind him. The county administrator and two of the county team members were in the hall; the county administrator was holding a stack of the revised proposals. Glances were exchanged quickly as the mediator shut the door. "Did you just come to bring over the copies?" the mediator asked. "Yes," the administrator replied, "but do they want to talk with us about it?" The mediator, as noted earlier, felt a strong motive to keep the two sides apart because of the potentially explosive matter of the city's special attorneys being present in the meeting. His guess was that if the county people entered the room, the talks (and the possibility of an agreement that night) were certain to break down. "Well," the mediator said, "I think they understand the changes pretty well." There was a pause, then the administrator said, "We just came over to bring the copies." The mediator offered his thanks and they moved off down the hall. (The next day, the mediator discovered that the county group had correctly guessed the reason the mediator did not have them enter the meeting. "We figured out what you were up to!" they told the mediator the next morning.)

The mediator re-entered the meeting room. Some of the city group were amazed that the county had delivered the copies already signed. The city now saw itself in a somewhat advantaged position because its surmise was that the county was eager to reach settlement that night. Attention focused back on the issue and continued, sometimes painfully, until almost 3:00 A.M.

At that point the mayor proposed that the city have the mediator poll the county side by telephone and tell them that the city was willing to settle "tonight if a majority of the county board would vote to change the wording from 'may' to 'must.'" The mediator was rather reluctant to do this, but it did seem that the agreement was now hinging on this issue. Although he did not judge it to be a major matter of substance, there did seem to be a great deal of feeling around it—a bit due to their having to meet while the county team slept. Hence, the mediator went to a private office and began telephoning the county board members. It was now after 3:00 A.M. Each county board member was able to say clearly that there could be no agreement to a change without a board meeting to discuss it; it was not clear that any of the board members clearly understood—through the sleep-clouded haze of their voices— exactly what was the issue or what their own personal position on it was.

The mediator reported the results of the poll and told the city group that he felt the phone discussions had gone badly because the county people were sleepy and confused after having been roused from bed in the middle of night. He went on to say that the intensity of this issue for the city was somewhat puzzling to him; this issue of the city's demand to be able to renegotiate the revenue sharing formula had never been part of the revenue sharing negotiations. Moreover, he said that the issue had never been brought up by the county in any form. The city manager acknowledged these assertions and went on to say that this issue could easily be delicately manipulated into the details of the revenue sharing study to favorably reflect their position. This statement seemed persuasive to the group because others expressed support for it. At last a firm consensus formed: They had decided that this issue was not really an issue after all.

Attention turned to the paragraph concerning the escape clause. The city attorney took the lead here and expounded a conservative point of view about the possibility that the city would be in a badly compromised position if a court denied the agreement and the county thereby could escape from the revenue sharing (the city would thus have experienced a substantial delay in the resolution of its needs, resulting in additional city costs). Again, the discussion turned to whether or not the county had been negotiating in good faith—if it could be trusted. (One council member adamantly insisted to the end that it could not.) The nature of this discussion was, like the one surrounding the earlier provision, primarily emotional in tone for a time. Ultimately, discussion focused on the more technical point of the probability that the court might deny the agreement.

Discussion continued on this subject until the mediator explained, as he had before, that from his perspective this whole situation seemed strange. He had heard each side questioning the good faith of the other over the same concept—a revenue sharing study—for weeks. Perhaps neither side truly wanted to settle with the other, but if the sides wanted to settle on anything, it seemed that this was to seek revenue sharing. At this point the city's outside attorneys spoke. In effect, they rendered an authoritative legal opinion about the wording of the new legislation. They made the point that the legislation specified that "the court shall be limited in its decision to either affirming or denying the voluntary agreement and shall have no authority . . . to amend or change the terms or conditions." They offered the opinion that given this language, it would be truly extraordinary, virtually inconceivable even, that a court would deny an agreement. They noted that the rules of evidence imposed by such a provision put a very strong prejudice on the side of affirming the agreement. This statement seemed, decisively, to settle the escape clause question. The group moved to accept the proposal and have the mayor sign it.

The agreement seemed to be imminent, but one matter remained: the county's proposal for how it was to be announced, which the mediator had deliberately chosen not to raise until now. When the city heard that the county wished the announcement to be made outside the city (at the state library) just prior to the commission's hearings, they reacted with subdued anger. Although they did not feel that they themselves would be compromised by the arrangement, they saw it as one more instance of relentless pressing for advantage on the part of the county. Quickly they devised an alternative plan—one that they believed was statesmanlike in nature and that the county could not refuse. It was important to the city that the agreement be announced within the bounds of the city, but they acknowledged it needed to be on more or less neutral territory. Hence, they proposed that the press conference be held at the entrance to the university in the city. They instructed the mediator to propose this location to the chairman of the county board by telephone.

When the county board chairman came to the telephone for the second time that night it was almost daybreak. The mediator first told him that an agreement had been reached, but that a problem had developed over how to hold the press conference. After describing the city's alternative proposal, the mediator made a strong and urgent pitch to the chairman to accept the city's idea and to make the decision on his own, right then, so that the agreement could be brought to closure. The chairman was at first unwilling to do this, but after further insistence by the mediator he agreed.

Upon hearing of the county's reaction, the city side was surprised and delighted. Spirits rose dramatically, one council member brought out a bottle of champagne, and toasts were made. One councilmember was not happy about the agreement, but nonetheless deferred to the mayor's wishes.

The mediator then went back to his hotel and placed a long list of telephone calls: first to the county administrator (who reported that he had said a prayer for the agreement before retiring) and then to the various newspapers and radio and television stations in the area that would want to attend the press conference. After this was done, time for the conference was nearing, so he went to the county administrative office building. Calls were coming into the office staff from the county board members, who had heard word of the agreement and were confused and even in states of consternation about the arrangements for the press conference. (When the mediator saw them later at the commission hearings, however, none of this was expressed; there were only congratulations and general good feelings all around.)

At the press conference the mediator distributed the following prepared press release:

From: Orion White: State Appointed Mediator in the Virginia County Annexation-Immunity Case. Roger Richman, the other State appointed mediator in the case and I, wish to commend the governing bodies of the City and the County, as well as the County Administrator and the

City Manager and the City and County Attorneys, for the time, diligence, and plain hard work that they have put into making this agreement. We feel that this agreement is in the public interest and that it is one more indication that responsible local leadership can cooperate to save taxpayers money and to keep control of the fate of local governments at the local level.

Analysis: Various Conclusions

There is typically ambivalence about using case studies as the basis for theoretical generalization or even speculation. On the one hand, they have great strength in providing a richness of data that no other methodological approach to the social world can match. On the other hand, the very richness of their data usually reveals that any particular case has such distinctive, if not unique, aspects about it that it seems to be a very tenuous base from which to draw general patterns.

Then there is the problem of the case data. The dilemma that case study writers often find most difficult is where to draw the line in presenting the data. Usually research involvement through case studies is so deep and wide that the writer has available far more data than even the most closely involved reader would ever be interested in seeing: the so-called seed catalogue problem. To avoid this situation the writer may "cull" and "weed out" data in the process of organizing the presentation of the study. However, if this process is carried too far, the interested reader will not be able to achieve the vicarious experiencing through which case studies provide the immediate and practical learnings that they alone among social science literature have to offer.

This dilemma is more complicated if the case study describes events that are contemporary or even recent and if the actors involved still have very real ego and career stakes on the line. In such instances the data must be selected further, with an eye to protecting the privacy of the actors who participated and cooperated in the conduct of the research.

All these factors came into play in this case, and the reader is asked to bear this in mind as he or she reflects on the various conclusions presented in this final section. Furthermore, the author wishes to emphasize that these conceptual observations are offered as tentative or speculative insights, and from the most modest of postures. What they reflect, as much as anything else, is the author's own felt experience as an actor—albeit one somewhat removed from the events of the case. From this general and tentative view, four general conclusions appear.

The Inevitable Variability of the Role of the Mediator

It is doubtless good mediation practice to define specifically as much as possible the role the mediator will play in a negotiation; this practice cannot be done in any certain or stabilizing way because of the dynamics of negotiations, which all the participants in this case seemed to realize. At some points in phase 2, in which there was prolonged back and forth haggling, the mediators occasionally exhibited high profile behavior. For example, these behaviors included grabbing away the marking pen from a team member (in a caucus session) to prevent him from redrawing the annexation line frivolously, confronting the parties directly about their personal behavior during negotiations, and almost revealing to one side the outline of an offer that the other side might be willing to accept. By contrast, examples of low profile behavior by the mediators include their occasional disregard of an apparently pointless strategy formulating session or venting of anger in nonconstructive ways. In other words, the mediators' behavior ranged from highly active to highly passive (behavior outside the range of behavior specified as appropriate in their contract). These extremes of behavior were reactions to particular situations. As long as their behavior stayed within the definition of the situation held by the participants, however, it was deemed appropriate. In many instances such behavior was certainly helpful in keeping the negotiations productive. If, on the other hand, their behavior overstepped these bounds, any number of the participants could have invoked the original contract and brought the mediators into serious question. To take the safe route and stay strictly and consistently within the bounds of the contract is, though, either to compromise seriously or block the mediators' potential for effectiveness.

It seems that setting an initial contract or definition of what the mediator's role is going to be is useful. For one thing, clients expect such an action; in addition to meeting this expectation, a contract gives clients a sense that the mediator knows what he or she is doing, understands the negotiation process, and will be able to structure and contain negotiations within productive channels. However, over the long run of day-to-day vicissitudes of the negotiations process, the contract will be forgotten, or not believed, or both.

Mediators are not exempt from the charges (implicit and explicit) of untrustworthiness that tend to permeate the air of conflict-laden situations. Typically, both sides will at times view the mediator as favoring the other side. (The goal of the effective mediator indeed is to ensure that both sides, rather than only one, feel this at some point.) In playing his or her role, therefore, the mediator must use the contract only as a point of reference and base actual behavior in the negotiations on the concrete reality of the negotiational situation as it unfolds. The only operative rule, in the end, is not to commit a disastrous error. The mediator's role is intrinsically and inevitably stressful.

The Persistent Influence of Feeling Issues

It was suggested in the introduction to this case that the city and the county represented two rather strikingly different subcultural value sets—values that define not only attitudes toward government but also lifestyle and personal style. This difference—the county representing country people and country life and the city representing small-scale, problematic urban areas—established a context in which mutual trust and interpersonal tension became the most pervasive single issue or force structuring the course of these negotiations. Even though the talks in the face-to-face setting were typically civilized, if not genteel, the people on each side simply did not have much faith in the people on the other side. Perhaps the most accurate way to state this is that each side saw the other in terms of very compelling psychological projections. Hence, the interpersonal issues (except for one or two instances between the attorneys for each side) stayed very much beneath the surface and in the background. The mediators did point out certain linguistic tangles in which the two sides sometimes got caught, but it was not sufficient to surface these issues and it did not seem possible that there was any appropriate way to do so. The context—annexation talks are the furthest thing from an encounter group!—and certainly the personalities did not allow for it.

In addition to the feelings generated by psychological images of the other side, the self-image held by each side produced feelings that influenced the talks. As remarked in the presentation of the case, the county saw itself in a position analogous to that of the American Indian—a party with a superior power (in this case the legal point to sue for annexation under conditions in which cities are expected to grow) was moving in on them to confiscate their land. It was evident at a number of times in the talks (occasions in which the county declared that it was seeking a reservation so it could develop a facility protected from further encroachment) that the county felt the city would potentially and eventually take away all the county's land except for the useless sections of it.

The city held a similar self-deprecating image of itself. They saw themselves as beleagured urbanites who were being beset with problems that were becoming acute and for which they either did not possess or have access to the resources needed. Two or three times during the talks, the city team members discussed the idea of simply turning in their charter as a city and letting the county have all the land. "If they [the County] don't believe our problems are real," the dialogue went, "then let them try to run this city and see!"

These feelings put both parties in a posture of needing acceptance, appreciation, and a supportive attitude. Because both parties could not or would not meet these needs, the feelings went unvented and unrelieved. It is only a bit of an overstatment to say that the lack of opportunity for expression of these feelings led to the county's malady of a mild form of paranoid suspiciousness and to the city's projection that the county groups was hidebound and insensitive.

Closely related to this issue was the issue of the land itself. Annexation-immunity disputes must initially and ostensibly be focused on the question of land—that is, where the annexation line shall be drawn. Land seems to carry a specially loaded archetypal symbolism with it, which is a distinctive part of the negotiations process. The fact that it is land that is the focus of negotiation generates specific feelings of ownership, protectiveness, possessiveness, and, on the other side, conquest and acquisition. It seems not simply by chance that the metaphors of war and international politics crop up in the conversations of participants in these cases. Admittedly, much of this language is due to the legal structure creating city-county separation (as documented in Chapter 2), however, that division of land is involved also heavily figures in the picture. It is not a large exaggeration to characterize annexation disputes as being very much like the clash of culture and nationality that sometimes occurs in international politics. This explanation in part accounts for the ambivalence that these parties had about the meaning of consolidation to them and the hesitations that they had, at least implicitly, about moving into a joint revenue sharing agreement. If revenue sharing truly meant moving toward one government for the whole area, they were not certain they wanted to take part in a change of that nature.

The Peculiarity of the Problem-Solving Phase

One of the most firm generalizations that has emerged from the experience of mediated settlement of annexation cases in Virginia is that the parties begin to move toward agreement when (1) they are able to reveal their bottom line positions to each other and (2) the focus of the talks broadens to include items that initially were not considered or were only ancillary to the main issues so that a package of tradeoffs can be put together that allows both parties to feel satisfied. This pattern was illustrated in this case to the extent that it was only when each side revealed their bottom line position that the emotional climate changed in a positive direction that provided for their moving toward settlement. This case differed from the pattern in other ways, however. The revelation of the bottom line was not done either under a condition of growing trust or with an indication of an increased willingness to come to terms with the other party. Rather, it was the emotive declaration of both parties: "This is the line from which we will not retreat." It is the peculiarity of this case that the double-back-up line idea allowed both parties to make such a declaration without its having a negative effect. (In fact it had a positive effect.) The back-up-line idea was a simple way of mechanically ensuring that the other side could be trusted. Hence, a true negotiated rapport never developed, nor did it need to develop for the talks to proceed to a successful conclusion.

As a result, there was no typical problem-solving phase—that is, the problem solving did not extend through much time. Indeed it was almost momentary. Although it is true that some ancillary issues were brought in subsequent to creation of the back-up-line idea—issues such as protection of the county's public works facility—no true problem solving occurred. The back-up-line idea settled the land question, and the rest of the matter was deferred to the consultant's study—these briefly deliberated solutions compose the problem-solving stage. It is safe to say that the agreement the problem solving supported was only an agreement to carry out an objective study.

The Autonomous Nature of the Negotiations Process

As noted from the outset, this study has conceptualized the events in this case as proceeding through the five stages, or phases, identified in chapter six as characteristic of annexation cases of this type. We have seen that this stage conceptualization does afford a reasonably accurate way of viewing the unfolding of the case if we adjust for the fact that the stages might not occur in segments of time that are equal in length or cosmetically the same as in other cases. The third stage—the problem-solving stage—is the primary exception in this regard. At a structural level, however, this pattern does seem to describe a generic dynamic that animates these cases. Problem solving in this case did not occur for as long as it has in other cases, nor did it occur in precisely the same way as in other cases. Nonetheless, it did happen, and it happened in a manner that at a fundamental level was like other cases.

Hence, we might speculate that what we have described as stages is an autonomous structural pattern revealing that, at their foundation, negotiations have a life of their own. They operate beyond the conscious control and beneath the awareness of the parties involved in acting them out. The rather amazing thing about this case is that any settlement at all occurred, given the emotional distance separating the two sides.

The parties were carried along by the process. In a real sense, the process itself effected the resolution, leaving the parties in a relationship to each other that they probably did not really expect, but to which they can and will probably adjust to (and which might very well work out in the long run). The research literature of small groups has long shown that a structural dynamic of just this sort underlies and governs the developments of groups from the time they form to the time they accomplish their task. Conflicts within families, between the generations of child and parent, perhaps work out (when they do work out) according to such an underlying dynamic.

If indeed it is true that negotiations are controlled by an underlying structural dynamic—the implications seem to be rather profound. One such implication is that research on the negotiations process could well focus on furthering our understanding of this structural pattern, rather than upon negotiation behaviors and the corollary matter of how to be effective at negotiating, especially in the sense of how to win. In addition, it would seem that the conceptual orientation and research methods of enthnomethodology could well be applied in the field of research on the negotiations process. If we could develop a good understanding of this dynamic, underlying pattern, then we could move on to identify the types of interventions that mediators can employ to help the process achieve transition from one stage to the next. (Such identifications have been made for facilitators of small groups.) That structural patterns— when and where they operate—do set the basic direction of events in human affairs does not mean that participants in these affairs are simply passive ciphers. The negotiating agents must do the hard and active work of authentically engaging the other side at every step and in each concrete moment of the talks. Mediators, for their part, must not merely retreat to the secure confines of a stably defined role from which they simply operate a number of standard interventions. Rather, sometimes they must walk a razor's edge of appropriateness and intuitively react to the situation so that it can progress.

In the end the best settlements are probably those that emerge (as opposed to being constructed). Assuming this is true, the main responsibility of the mediator is to the process of negotiating itself. It is the process that must be trusted; it is the process that the mediator must represent. Participants in negotiations and mediators should seek to understand the process as far as possible; yet, they are perhaps best advised that the negotiations process is enhanced to the greatest extent if all participants simply live through it as authentically as possible.

5

The Dynamics of
Intergovernmental Negotiations

The great paradox of the mediation role is that, even though negotiations are universally considered to be highly rational, they are driven
by nonrational dynamics. The dominant impression is that, when people
sit down to negotiate something, they focus on their self-interest—that
is, on their immediate stakes in the matter under consideration. They
are, we tend to think, calculating how they can best serve their own
interests through the negotiation process. This description suggests a
highly calculated, cognitive, emotionally cool image of negotiation. We
speak of people as being shrewd negotiators, implying that they have
a sharp eye in weighing the possible outcomes of negotiated deals.

Anyone who has participated in neogitations, either as party to them
or as a mediator, has probably found that the process seldom fits this
rational image. Emotional factors frequently form the baseline along
which negotiations proceed. The interpersonal dynamics between the
parties can sometimes be the critical factor that turns the process toward
successful settlement or toward breakdown and, in many cases, the
courtroom. One consequence of this gap between the image and reality
of negotiation is that the mediator, on the one hand, must appear as a
hardheaded realist oriented toward the stakes for which the parties are
playing, and, on the other hand, must have the skills to intervene in
the softer, affective side of the process—that is, to effectively deal with
the emotions and interpersonal tangles that can snarl and stop negotiations.

A Conceptual Model

This chapter presents a conceptual model of the dynamics of the
negotiation process as it has operated in city-county boundary disputes
in Virginia. Its purpose is to show the complex interplay of cognitive
and emotional elements that occur in negotiations and that place the
mediator in the paradoxical position previously described. Although the

examples here involve boundary dispute negotiations, they provide insights by which mediators in other negotiations can be more effective in moving disputes toward successful, nonlitigious resolutions.

The conceptual model is based on the sequence of each negotiating party's positions. The model shows what happens at each stage as the parties formulate a presentation of what they seek from the negotiations (see Figure 5.1). As might be surmised, this sequence begins inside each party—in the intrapsychic realm—and moves through interpersonal exchanges to public pronouncements that become the substance of the negotiation talks. The course of the presentations is affected by myriad structural and more capricious influences. The road from "wants" to stated positions is a long and tortuous one.

The Source Point: Vital Interests or Wants

Clinical psychologists have remarked that if God had given people the capacity to know what they wanted all the time, therapists and counselors could not stay in business. This point is relevant for understanding negotiations. At the very core of negotiations is a sense of vital interests, desires, or wants. Each side is seeking the satisfaction or achievement of these wants through the vehicle of negotiation. These wants make up the psychological bottom line of each party. The term bottom line captures the essence of stakes as they are felt at the psychological level—namely, a point exists past which each party will not go in making concessions, a hard and fast limit to compromise that bounds the negotiation talks.

Nonetheless, though stakes are felt to be immutable, it is almost always difficult, if not impossible, for the parties in a dispute to translate these vital interests into concrete negotiational positions. As the psychologists' remark implies, what people must often do in their personal lives is conduct nonfocused discussions (sometimes with therapists) through which psychological wants or interests can be recognized and stated as practical agendas. The same is true in negotiated disputes. The parties definitely have bottom lines, but these are generally ambiguous and vague. Indeed, when the parties can carry their discussion to the level of vital interests, negotiations acquire the special texture so vital to constructing the package of payoffs to each side that composes a settlement. Again, in negotiations we are faced with a paradox: We would expect the parties to become most rigid when they get down to discussing their bottom-line interests, but at this point the process maximizes the potential for creative dialogue.

That is why identification with and dialogue around positions, though probably inevitable, are so difficult and progress so haltingly. The

Figure 5.1
Negotiation Dynamics

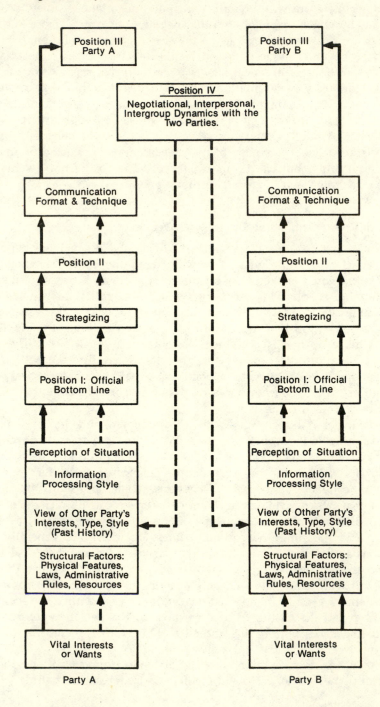

stereotype negotiation ends by splitting the difference; yet few disputes of any complexity or scale ever get settled in this way. Such matters require the synergy of true negotiation, a synergy that occurs when authentic contact about vital interests is achieved.

The lack of clarity with which a party perceives its own stakes derives from a number of sources. One is that the situation being addressed is seldom clear; usually several alternatives are available. Apart from extreme choices, the decision among options may be ambiguous, affected more by sentiments about what other parties are doing than by the merits of each alternative.

Another reason for our lack of clarity regarding our wants is that as a culture we are not attuned to looking at wants; rather, we are more oriented toward looking at what we ought to do or should do. Hence, we often seek to define wants in terms of rights or other imperatives. There may or may not be a correspondence between the underlying psychological want and the externally defined value. People sometimes change homes because they ought to now that they have achieved a certain status in life. They consider a new home as more appropriate to their position, even though they may not actually want (or be happier in) the new home.

The third and most powerful reason that our wants are so obscure to us is that our culture—capitalistic and competitive as it is—teaches us not to identify and seek what we want but to get as much as we can. As E. L. Doctorow put it in his novel *Ragtime:* "In America, it is not enough to win, others must lose." Given this orientation, it is irrelevant to specify one's underlying vital interests. Since the objective is to best the other party, attention is turned outward, toward the situation (or game), and energy becomes focused on how to outdo the other side. Some observers of mediated settlements, especially attorneys, have wondered how the parties involved can be happy with the outcome, because there can always be a nagging feeling that more could have been gotten in court. Even if this is true and the parties suspect it, mediated settlements probably still produce a curious type of satisfaction—that is, for our culture. Both parties are almost always relieved to have the dispute done with—this is a clear mutual payoff—and they often do get what they wanted. Although they do not know how to appreciate this fully sometimes, it is a satisfactory outcome at a psychological level.

Unfortunately, this attitude seems to structure conflicts so that things must get worse before they can get better. That is, parties initiate their discussions by stating positions—positions that they claim are reasonable and as far as they can possibly go but that are in truth grossly in preparation for "horsetrading." Parties almost always feel this process is beneath them, but they do not know any alternative; nor can they envision one, so strong are our cultural images about how negotiations proceed. As a consequence, the present model of negotiation dynamics begins where vague psychological wants start to interact with external consideration. It is here that a party to a dispute begins to formulate a position that can be brought to the negotiating table.

Structural Factors

The conscious formation of a negotiational position starts with the structure of the external situation as perceived by the attorneys, professional staff, and politicians. It is against reality that the desired outcome of getting as much as one can is initially reflected. It is typical in decision situations in this culture for the parties involved to turn first to the facts and proceed from there. Parties to annexation-immunity disputes are no exception. In these cases, for example, attention is often focused on the physical setting, the actual topography of the land involved. In some instances topographical or physical features such as watershed lines, riverbeds, interstate highways, or mountains indicate definite limitations or opportunities in the formation of position. Another aspect of the external situation is the relevant laws and administrative rules. This factor is the major one conditioning the process of these disputes. The money available for litigating the dispute is a third substantial element bearing on the parties' concept of what position to take.

A second consideration in the formation of a negotiational position is each side's view of the other side—particularly the other side's governing board. Here assessments of character come in, and the necessity or possibility for reason, persuasion, intimidation, or dismay is weighed. One side attempts to read the other side's interests and get a sense of what they are up to. These judgments typically are rather personal, and past experiences with the people involved are inevitably brought up. At this point the emotional postures of each side toward the other are set, and these postures will be carried into the negotiation sessions.

This set of information and perceptions is worked through in a context that is structured by the personal styles of the members of each side. People process information differently: some are predominantly fact oriented, some are more receptive to abstract argument, others tend to focus on the relationships involved in a situation, and others are primarily interested in creatively finding a breakthrough. A group of people, formed into a negotiating team, will operate in a dominant style that is characteristic of the majority of its members or of its leader. This factor—how groups process information as they work—operates implicitly, but its power in affecting the course and outcome of negotiation talks cannot be overestimated.

Positions and Strategies:
The Substance of Negotiation Dynamics

Undefined vital interests, molded by the structural considerations described in the previous section, emerge as each party's primary negotiating position or official bottom line. This is identified as Position I, and in boundary negotiations it is typically expressed as a line on a map that is kept secret throughout negotiations—even from the mediators, who may be sent out of the room when it is brought out and used as a point of reference for the talks. Position I defines the line from which there will be no retreat. It is usually not seen as defining what is wanted as much as indicating the least that will be accepted. The definition of Position I plays at least two important functions in setting up the dynamics of the negotiations. First, by defining its bottom line, the team establishes its identity and is drawn together into a unit. Second, the clear definition of the bottom line serves to protect the team from itself. It can go into the rough-and-tumble of negotiations knowing that it knows where to stop. The line is insurance that the team will not inadvertently give away too much. Like any insurance, this type affords a measure of security that can promote flexibility or openness in the negotiations themselves.

A party will not, of course, enter a negotiation by bidding its bottom-line position at the outset. Rather, it will utilize its skill and its assessment of the situation to formulate a strategy for approaching the negotiation in a way that will maximize its outcomes. This calculated attempt leads to a second position, Position II, which typically is far different from Position I. Indeed, for strategic reasons, Position II may be deliberately overdrawn (although it will be rational to the initiating party) and hence may communicate little or nothing about the party's true position. It is only a small overstatement to say that Position II is looked upon as a device for disorienting the other side so as to open opportunities for perhaps serendipitous gains.

We cannot say, however, that even Position II, as defined by the proposing party, is communicated to the other side. That is, inside the chambers of the party that formulates it, it is one thing, but when embodied and presented to the other side in the negotiation setting, it necessarily becomes something else. Making and responding to proposals are critical points in negotiations, and one reason why mediators seek to set norms structuring these events. A variety of communication formats and techniques are available to a team presenting a position, ranging from the heurisitc, informal probe delivered outside the meeting room to the formal speech presented at a joint session of the governing boards. The medium, if it does not in fact become the message, at least comes to bear heavily in the definition of it. Illustrations of this effect will be provided later; the transformations of meaning that take place are sometimes marvelous to witness. The most frequent one is that a proposal intended to invite and initiate a series of bids back and forth becomes in the hands of the presenter a rigid or dogmatic demand that insults the receiving party and brings the talks to the edge of collapse.

Hence, Position II, as and when presented, becomes still something else—namely, Position III. It is Position III to which the receiving party responds. At this point the stage is set for a rich and complex pattern of intergroup and interpersonal dynamics to begin. Since the presenting party most likely does not see the distinction between Position II and Position III (they are unaware that a redefinition of it occurred in the presentation), they are likely to be puzzled by the response of the receiving side. As a result the presenter's subsequent response will be partly confused, leading possibly to suspicions on the party of the other side, then mutual suspicion, and so on. As these dynamics proceed, two further effects occur: First, yet another position, Position IV, emerges from the negotiational dynamics. Second, actual experiences in the negotiations feed back to the two parties' perceptions of each other. These modified perceptions can lead to a redefinition of the situation, then a revision of strategy and of Position II—and so on—in a continuing loop or cycle, all occurring beneath the surface and creating important but unacknowledged influences on the talks.

It should be clear from the model that negotiation in intergovernmental boundary cases (and other cases) is by no means the rational, straightforward process depicted in our stereotypes about negotiation. Myriad nonrational factors come into play at every point. The purpose here is to use this model for discussing how mediators can understand, work with, and intervene in these dynamics so that the capricious effects they tend to create in negotiations can be reduced. A subsidiary purpose is to illustrate and document these dynamics from experience in a number of annexation-immunity cases.

The Psychosocial Dynamics of Negotiations

We must recall that the mediator, in order to build and maintain credibility, is best advised to emphasize the concrete—or more technical or structure-oriented—aspects of the role. The effectiveness of a mediator is typically undermined if the mediator presents himself or herself as some sort of communications or interpersonal relations specialist. To extend this point, we note again that mediators are not therapists, which is ironic because perhaps the most helpful thing mediators could do in annexation-immunity cases is conduct a kind of group therapy session with each side to distill as clearly as possible its vital interests. The limits of appropriateness, however, dictate that the most the mediator can legitimately do is work at the surface of the negotiations—at the level of intergroup dynamics and with individuals. The mediator must be circumspect, however, and where possible operate under cover of substantive discussion. At the same time, though, it must be noted that as a case proceeds, more actions can be taken at the deeper levels (for example, the levels of defining vital interests and redefining the situation). Therefore, most of the time the mediator must pay heed to one definition of the role while acting from a much broader definition of it.

From this broader role definition, the mediator can work both to (1) establish valid relationships with individuals on the two sides, so that the individuals feel that the mediator fully understands their point of view and appreciates them as people and (2) develop membership, in the sense of a role presence, with each of the parties. The mediator must work past being a stranger in the midst of the two sides.

First Level: Vital Interests

In examining the details of negotiation dynamics, let us begin again at the basic level, the area of vital interests and wants. Since each party will feel that it has a clear definition of these—as represented in its (secret) Position I—it will usually not be easy for a mediator to focus attention on clarifying these and developing a coherent, cohesive viewpoint on them. This matter can be approached at least obliquely in a number of ways, however. For example, one of the major contributions a mediator can make is in mediating the inevitable intrateam disputes over position and strategy.

In many cases negotiations become stalled because one or both of the negotiating teams are too entangled in their own internal disputes to deal effectively with the other party. By working through these intrateam disputes the mediator paves the way for better communication with the other party, often resulting in clarification of vital interests and increased openness. In caucus sessions the mediator can sometimes help each side clarify and discuss its vital interests as a way of working toward intrateam cohesion and harmony.

A second way of working at this basic level of vital interests and wants is to ask each party to state what it believes to be the broad vital interests of the other side and to compare this statement with another statement by each party regarding its own vital interests. By so doing, of course, the party will have to reflect on its own general and vital interests.

A third technique is for the mediator, at appropriate points, to explain to a party what the mediator has determined the party's vital interests to be based on what was said in the negotiations. Response to this feedback might lead to further clarification of the party's interests.

Second Level: Perception of the Situation

At the next level—how the party perceives and interprets the situation—the mediator can sometimes be much more directly active and potentially helpful. The setting for these interventions, of course, must be the caucus, or single-side meetings. Perhaps the most powerful type of intervention in this setting is for the mediator to communicate experiences in past cases or point out nuances of law, administrative procedure, or policy that lead the party to redefine the situation in such a way that options are opened up and possibilities for movement in new directions appear. Of course on technical points the parties will defer to their own technical experts. Also, no two cases are exactly alike, and the parties will be quick to remind the mediator that experience does not transfer fully. Hence, the mediator does face some definite limits in working at this level. Relevant information from other cases is useful and appropriate when it is offered simply as something to consider. In more technical areas, the mediator should restrict inputs to those that might inspire imaginative, creative thinking.

Another area for intervention by the mediator at this level is the matter of psychological projections toward the other team. Anyone who has worked much with groups knows that a great deal of the perception in intergroup relations is really projection—that is, the negative traits of one's own are imputed to the other side. This process accounts for perhaps most of the negative emotionalism and communications tangles that can characterize difficult negotiations.

One outstanding example was an instance in which a member of one negotiating team solemnly told the mediators, "We have decided that if they come in tonight with a proposal as ridiculous as our last one, we are going to walk out!"

In another instance, a party complained to the mediators that the other side was not negotiating in good faith, as evidenced by the fact that they had come to the negotiation session with a press release ready to pass out at the end of the evening. When the mediator pointed out that the speaker's own team had gone into the meeting with a prepared press release, he was somewhat taken back as he realized it was true. Nonetheless, he quickly (and defensively) retorted, "Well, but ours was only handwritten; they had theirs typed out!"

In some cases projections can be centered in interpersonal relations across teams and involve professional egos, making them particularly difficult to deal with. In one case the planning staffs of the two sides saw each other in precisely the same terms—as mostly incompetent sellouts to development interests. In another case the staff attorneys for the two sides described each other to the mediators in almost verbatim (and nearly scurrilous) language. It is important that the mediator have built something of a trust relationship, including informal channels of communication, with the parties before attempting to intervene in psychological projections. A humorous retort from the other side's point of view can often gently jar the subject into self-reflection. Working through projections is particularly difficult, as the sides will want the mediator to buy into and share its projections. Therefore, the mediator must be cautious, subtly using objective data from joint sessions—for example, statements from one side that are at odds with the other side's projections. It is sometimes remarkable to see the extent to which the two sides in a negotiation misperceive each other. Such problems can only be sorted out by helping each side, slowly, to stop projecting and come to a more accurate sense of the other side.

Third Level: Communication Format and Technique

There are basically two types of strategy for the mediator to follow at the level of communication format and technique. At this level, the reader will recall, the parties are presenting their strategic position (Position II) and are altering it in the process. One strategy is simply to be aware of the miscommunication that typically occurs at this level and deal with it in situ as it occurs. Techniques used to this end include caucusing and providing feedback or by process interventions such as asking the receiving team to restate the position being presented.

In one case a curious reverse example of miscommunication at this step occurred. One side presented a position openly, hoping to evoke a counterproposal. The receiving team retorted arrogantly that the proposal did not please them and a new proposal would have to be made before they would respond. An emotional blowup, complete with cursing, ensued. The mediators made a few process interventions, but these were not what led to the increased understanding that resulted. The emotionalism of the incident itself led the team receiving the proposal to believe the authenticity of the other teams' desire to negotiate in good faith. This example well illustrates how the medium is the message in negotiations and how the manner of presentation is often the critical factor in communicating to the other side. By being sensitive to what is happening during a presentation, a mediator can help move the parties' understanding of each other closer to their intentions.

As mentioned earlier, however, the more typical problem at this level is that a party will formulate a position intended to lead to a counterproposal, to which they can respond to in turn, and so on, but then they present the position in such a way that the receiving side reads it as a final (and therefore unacceptable) offer.

In order to ward off such misunderstandings, the mediator can (1) ask the side after it has formulated its position to consider how they wish to communicate it so that they will get the intended response or (2) actually take the presenting member aside and coach him or her on how to go about the presentation. Even then, the problem may arise. In one case the presenting side decided to run an idea up the flagpole to see the other party's response. The mediator coached the presenter, suggesting a low-key, if not casual, introduction and a tentative statement of the position. The presenter acknowledged that such an approach fitted his side's objective at that point and agreed to follow the suggestions. However, when he took the floor to present his team's position, he began with a long prefatory statement that he ardently hoped the proposal he was about to make would be accepted because "in the spirit of good faith and in hope of gaining agreement," his team members had pushed themselves as far as they could go in making concessions and had reached the point where "their basic goals are in danger of being compromised." The mediator sat dismayed as the inevitable reaction unfolded.

Two other techniques mediators can use to cope with the problem are to take over a team's proposition and present it to the other side as his own or simply to carry one side's proposal to the other as a messenger. In either case the mediator can exercise complete control over how a proposal is presented.

Fourth Level: Negotiation Dynamics

Mediators can be most active at the surface level of negotiations— the interpersonal communication events that constitute the negotiation dynamics that lead to Position IV, the position actually communicated to the other team as the talks proceed. A great deal happens at this level, and one of the major responsibilities of the effective mediator is to be conscious of and track the effects of as much of these dynamics as possible. In one case, for example, a member of a negotiating team, the mayor of the city involved in a dispute, failed through oversight to shake hands with a member of the county's team. This slight, though inadvertent, so angered and disturbed the offended member of the county team that he did not get over it through the entire course of the talks. The mediators made this an object of considerable discussion, however, and amends were made that were heard at least by other members of the county team.

In another instance the mayor of the city had his team meet with mediators prior to introducing them to the city council. A few members of the council arrived early and entered the meeting room, whereupon the mayor asked them to step outside and wait until the appointed time for the council to meet. Both the mediators present were immediately aware of the effects this move would have, but since this was their initial meeting in the case, they felt they had not yet laid a sufficient base of legitimacy for intervening. The results were nearly disastrous, for the negotiating team never gained the full trust and cooperation of the council.

A second area in which mediators can definitely help is the management of emotion through increasing the participants' awareness of how the language they use affects feelings on both sides. That is, in discussing the issues of a dispute, the parties will frequently employ language that they feel is innocuous but that will actually put off or even inflame the other team.

In one case the two sides had attempted to carry on talks without mediation help for several weeks. They had even, wisely, agreed on a set of general ground rules for the talks. Yet, when the mediators were brought in, the sides had become so hostile that they were barely on speaking terms. After reestablishing talks and observing for a while, it became clear to the mediators that both sides were doing two things. First, they were using—innocently—a number of emotionally loaded phrases. Second, they were introducing irrelevant topics that were heating up the talks so much that neither side could continue to function in a rational manner. For example, county team members frequently referred in the coolest, most objective tone to their desire to protect a particular area of land from annexation. The city team visibly rankled at the word "protect," for they read into it a variety of negative implications about city government. (The county, of course, believed some of these implications, but the point is that constantly stimulating such reactions on the city side impeded the talks.)

In addition, each side felt that it had been responsible for bringing about the commercial development that existed in the areas adjacent to the city that were under dispute. Hence, whenever one side referred to "our development," argument ensued.

In another instance one side brought up an example from the past history of the negotiations that it felt demonstrated that the other side had deceived it. This charge was matched with a counterexample, which was in turn matched, and so on. In all, eight such exchanges were identified by the mediators and discussed in separate meetings with each side. The teams agreed that bringing them up added nothing to the talks, and they acknowledged how heavily loaded they were and how they had affected their interactions with the other team. Not only were the teams successful in virtually eliminating such remarks from their discussions, but they also showed an increased awareness of how their language affected the other side, often putting in hedges and provisos in their statements that were designed to ward off misunderstandings and consequent needless emotionality.

Another area in which the mediator can help is the efficiency of listening and its corollary, semantic tangles. Organizational research has amply documented that the efficiency of work-related communication (i.e., involving information about tasks) is astoundingly low. The same holds true in negotiation meetings. Sometimes parties simply do not hear each other, and other times they misunderstand; they are seldom able to get their messages to connect, as intended. In one negotiation at a key point, the mediator stopped a participant who was just beginning to respond to a statement from the other side and asked him to tell the other team what he understood the other side to have just said. Perplexed, he blurted out, "I don't have the slightest idea what they just said!" Mediators must track the dialogue of talks very closely and quickly interject probes, interventions, or clarifications that will prevent misunderstanding or improve comprehension. A great help can be provided here with only a small effort. Those engaged in the fray can use the help of an outside observer in identifying what they are both saying and hearing.

One of the early moves for the mediator is to establish a set of norms, ground rules, or negotiating conventions as a framework for the talks. The enforcement of these norms is perhaps the single most important thing the mediator can do to improve the dynamics of negotiations. In representing these norms the mediator is establishing himself or herself as the symbolic authority figure who defines appropriate behavior. This role is important more at the symbolic level than in actual practice because no mediator would get very far in actually issuing fiats about the behavior of the negotiators. That is, the presence of the mediator itself refers the talks out to the broader setting of society and government generally, where "reasoned discourse" and "fairness" are broadly accepted norms. Further, the mediator represents a norm of positive strategy formulation—that is, strategy concerned with how to achieve settlement. He or she is a counterweight to the tendency for parties in a dispute to move toward extreme positions. To the parties, the mediator must symbolize moderation and balance.

Although it may be disappointing, it is nonetheless true that lacking such an operative symbol, negotiation talks can quickly sink into the morass of interpersonal dynamics in which anything but reasoned discourse takes place. The negotiation setting is an unfamiliar, even normless place to the participants. As ethnomethodological studies have shown, in such circumstances people will seek to find benchmarks indicating what behaviors are appropriate. The mediator embodies such benchmarks, and they are expressed to a large extent through the norms he or she proposes for the negotiations. This symbolic impact is the main way in which the dynamics of the talks are structured. To play this role effectively, the mediator must take actions in the name of the norms sparingly and carefully yet firmly; these actions range from simply reminding the participants of a norm to calling a halt to the negotiations. A not unimportant side dimension is management of the physical arrangements for the joint sessions, for press announcements, and for any other meetings. The meeting ground is neutral territory and therefore it is appropriately the province of the mediator, who can take an active role in arranging it.

The most difficult aspect of the mediator's role, perhaps, is that he or she becomes privy to information about one side's position that cannot be divulged to the other side. No precise rules or even guidelines can be defined for dealing with this dimension of the role. However, one thing can be noted: Often in joint meetings one side will make hints or suggestions about its position that it does not wish to reveal explicitly for what it sees as strategic reasons. The mediator, by knowing what he or she does about that side's position, can recognize these hints as a veiled form of proposal making and can initiate an exploration of them by, for example, asking the receiving side to reflect on what it understands the signals to mean. This device can frequently open new lines of discussion without the slightest compromise of a team's position by the mediator.

In sum, although the level of negotiation dynamics is the surface level, and hence the least connected to the give-and-take that is the heart of the process, there is nonetheless a great deal that can be done at this level to both reduce negative factors and provide positive impetus to the proceedings. The payoffs make it well forth the effort required to track and work with these surface dynamics. In doing so, though, it is useful to try to avoid a number of actions. It bears repeating, in this context, that the mediator must make it a principle not to reveal information from one side to the other. Also, mediators must not fall into the trap of pressuring one side and not the other to compromise. This is simple advocacy and has nothing to do with mediation. The mediator is not an arbitrator or judge and should avoid this position even when the parties pressure him or her to assume it—as they are apt to do frequently. Last, although expertise can be shared with the sides, mediators are not consultants and must avoid offering authoritative analyses or opinions on the technical aspects of proposals.

Conclusion

This chapter has attempted to show, conceptually, some of the complexities that beset the negotiation process in annexation-immunity cases. These complexities often cause the position taken by each side to be understood by the other side in a way that is far different from the way the side exposing the position intended it to be understood. Vital interests are misunderstood between parties in the same way. A number of illustrations of these dynamics and effective mediator interventions were also described. Experience in negotiation shows that it is not the rational, objective process we so often think it to be. Rather, it must be regarded and dealt with as a complex, ever-changing, even volatile psychosocial process, even though we must pay homage to the image of it as rational.

By regarding the negotiating process in this way, the mediator can manage the caprice of the process, improve communication, and increase the comfort each side feels in dealing with the other. As comfort with the negotiating relationship grows, so does trust. The bottom-line payoff of mediation is that it nurtures the trust required as a foundation for the parties' moving to dialogue at the level of vital interests and wants. At this fundamental level the magic of negotiation produces a winning resolution for both sides even where it seemed initially that one must win and one must lose.

6

Mediator Roles
and Negotiation Structures

In the previous chapter we described various mediation activities as being based on the mediator's reading of dispute dynamics. In this chapter, we review the influence of negotiation structures on the conduct of the negotiation, identifying settings that condition the course of disputes and the roles and actions the mediator can adopt. Our premise is that mediation roles are significantly regulated by underlying structural phenomena—for example, by the parties' past interactions with each other and by their internal team organization (group structure and process), by the "space" given the mediator by the external framework of law and policy, and by other factors. In intergovernmental disputes these underlying structural factors assume particular relevance for two main reasons: (1) Structured negotiations and mediation roles are unfamiliar to public officials and (2) disputing local governments have no comparable organizational and behavioral models available that fit the organized negotiation situation. We have found that interjurisdictional negotiations often are relatively poorly organized, in part from the parties' ad hoc development of negotiating subarenas in their efforts to structure, order, and control the dispute. Consequently, we see that a key role for the intergovernmental mediator is to aid the disputants in developing the internal order of the negotiations, including the ordering of the issues and the communication processes between and within negotiating teams.

Our aim is to describe how the intergovernmental mediator functions in disputes at impasse—what his or her roles are and what factors affect different role dimensions (that is, what structural and functional conditions of intergovernmental disputes impose requirements on third-party neutrals). The material in this chapter is drawn from the case experiences in interjurisdictional boundary negotiations in Virginia. We have used this experience to develop the principles underlying the general model of structural factors and mediator roles that we describe. The development of this general model is the major objective of this chapter.

Background Factors in Intergovernmental Negotiations

A primary lesson of the experience in intergovernmental mediation in Virginia is that mediator roles vary with the changing context of evolving negotiations and that mediators must be prepared to act in emerging and uncertain environments. Our first task in discussing mediation roles, therefore, must be to describe the factors that condition the intergovernmental dispute environment.

Figure 6.1 identifies key background roles and factors affecting the framing of interjurisdictional disputes by local negotiators. The diagram shows that, apart from the formal setting for talks between localities, in which mediators may engage in traditional third-party neutral activities, a complex set of actors and structural factors exists that creates negotiation subarenas for disputants, in which individuals on each side make choices through group processes. The decisions made in these subarenas are crucial to the negotiation—whether formal negotiations will be held and what the fate of the negotiations will be once begun. In interjurisdictional disputes, therefore, mediators intent on engaging in the dispute as completely as possible will find themselves acting in each side's negotiation subarenas, thus extending themselves beyond the intermediary role in formal joint negotiations sessions. The following discussion specifies certain relationships and dynamics within local governments as they configure themselves for formal negotiations.

The horizontal dashed line in Figure 6.1 separates two governments (city and county) presented in the diagram as separate mirror images. This line and the mirror images suggest that local officials in disputes tend to deal with very similar internal processes when positioning themselves in a dispute stance. In adversarial situations they look away from each other, ignoring each other's interests, except to characterize them as trivial or, worse, as a plot against their own interests. The officials on the same side shape themselves into a group that acts separately from the other side, as if the other side existed only as an abstraction. Mediator analysis of the dispute situation thus begins with the reconnaissance of the parties' relations with each other; in most, but not all, dispute situations in which the mediator is called in, the parties are isolated in two armed camps with respect to the issues in dispute.

The Decision to Negotiate or to Litigate

Early in the development of an interlocal dispute, usually after direct staff-level negotiations have not been able to solve a problem, local governing boards may enter litigation either simply to force the issue

Figure 6.1
Negotiation Substructures: Background Factors and Roles

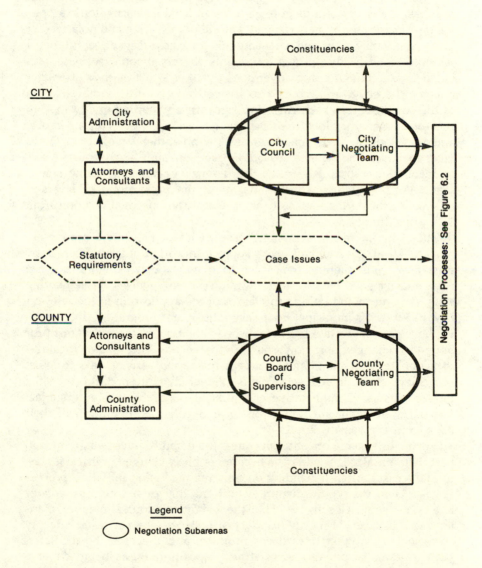

or because governing legislation requires court adjudication of the dispute (for example, court judgment is required in municipal boundary adjustments, as described in this book). The courts are regarded as a routine path for dispute settlement in interlocal matters; if issues are limited in scope and impact, such as the terms of an interjurisdictional contract, interlocal relations are generally unaffected. However, in cases in which the issues of a dispute go to vital, local concerns (for example, major resource allocation decisions), a spiral of escalation and polarization of the issues may occur and, consequently, may adversely affect interlocal relations. Specifically, local governments in this dispute scenario will begin to self-configure into adversarial postures—that is, they no longer relegate the adversarial context to their attorneys and to the isolation of the courtroom. In such cases local governing boards initially look in two directions—they look to their staffs to develop options on the issues, and they look to their constituencies for an indication of how far to take an adversarial stance. Based in part on staff analyses and recommendations, local governing boards may generate a public stance that reflects both their conclusions about the background of law and policy structuring the issues of the case and the informed reaction from their constituents.

The statutory requirements and case issues of Figure 6.1 are closely related. Local governments exist subject to conditions established by state law. Consequently, the issues in disputes between localities are regulated by state law, by state administrative agencies implementing state law, and by judicial interpretation of the application of the relevant law. In Virginia's municipal boundary adjustment program, for example, we have seen how state law established litigation as the mechanism for boundary changes and how changes in the law encouraged localities to negotiate settlements and to accept mediation as a process to assist in achieving negotiated settlements. Generally, interpretations of the pattern of state administrative and judicial policy in a dispute subject area have an important impact on local negotiators' definition of their options in a given dispute.

By the time mediators enter disputes, the disputes have usually moved past their initial stages and have become publicly charged political issues. In many cases, often depending on how the mediation initiation process is conducted, the typical dispute conditions that exist when a mediator enters a dispute closely resemble the conditions found in labor management disputes during the conduct of a strike. The parties are deeply suspicious of any act toward compromise, and they see the mediator, both in terms of power and of strategic positioning, as being either a useful or a negative influence upon their effective application of power in the situation. Thus the introduction of the mediator into a dispute at impasse, a dispute with a history, may be perceived by the parties as an infringement on their decided course of action of rejecting settlement on currently available terms and of spurning any negotiating policy. Certainly the mediator's entry into cases in which mediators have been previously absent is often contingent upon the advocacy of the mediation process by authority structures (state agencies and the courts) that regulate the dispute subject.

Local governments' decisions to participate in negotiations are often critically affected by their attorneys' predilections (to litigate or to negotiate) and analysis of the alternatives, given the context of the law and the policy of state administrative agencies. The initial case issues are derived from the conditions in the law that establish the rights and obligations of the parties and by the way the parties (or their attorneys) frame a course of action based on their reading of the law and its attendant procedures. One of the mediator's important tasks in the early stages of his or her entry into a case is to begin expanding the parties' participation in the issues by advocating looking at the issues in new ways—that is, moving from legalistic interpretations to the substance of the issues to be negotiated.

Other factors influencing the decision to negotiate surface in relationships between elected officials and their constituents. In important disputes each community's officials seek out and are influenced by their constituencies' views on the issues, as outlined in Figure 6.1. Because members of the city council or county board of supervisors typically represent a number of constituencies with different interests in the disputed issues, a more complex structure of relationships exists than that represented in the figure. For example, in several annexation negotiations in which local officials were elected by district rather than at large, the various effects of a proposed annexation on different districts resulted in elected officials representing some districts opposing negotiations while elected officials representing other districts were supporting negotiations. In some cases, directly affected representatives facing timely elections have rejected negotiations in order to campaign as fighters rather than as compromisers. Constituent expectations and demands obviously play a key role in negotiations involving elected officials. And the influence of constituencies operates in one important negotiation subarena: the local governing body. This body determines the policy for one disputing side; the individual elected officials that compose the body represent different affected constituencies and, consequently, they differ on the issues. They must work through their differences under the pressures of deciding how to manage the dispute— in particular, they must decide whether to try to negotiate or to litigate and they must select from alternative negotiating positions.

Substructures on Each Side

Governing boards do not often negotiate as a whole. They usually delegate negotiations to a group that includes a few elected officials, administrative officials and staff members (city manager or county administrator, department heads, and the local government's attorney), and outside expert consultants (for example, special counsel and other consultants with expertise in the dispute subject). Negotiating teams may be formally designated in disputes in which negotiations are formally undertaken; these teams are usually given somewhat ambiguous direction with respect to their discretion to make proposals without prior authorization by the full governing board. When a negotiating team is established, a negotiating subarena—between the team and the governing board—is inevitably also created (see Figure 6.1).

Negotiators are never given a carte blanche, and governing boards retain the right to reject proposals and settlements reached by their designated negotiators. However, because a negotiating team quickly gains special knowledge of the dispute situation and of the other side's positions it usually is able to bring along the full governing board to ratify suggested proposals and settlement conditions that the negotiators have developed. Yet in instances in which powerful individuals on the governing board are either not on a negotiating team or are not in favor of positions developed by the team, the full board or council may reject or severely modify positions taken by negotiators, either as a tactic or because of authentic doubts about these positions. Negotiators may question the other team's relationship with its governing board—namely, the other team's ability to sell a position to its governing board. In these situations, as in others, mediators are compelled to become involved in the subarena negotiations, both between the teams and their boards and in the deliberations within the board itself.

In Figure 6.1 we have identified two negotiating subarenas that structure the actual negotiation both prior to its initiation and throughout its course. Furthermore, we have specified the important linkage between the frame of law and policy that structures the case and the role of special attorneys and consultants as advisors and occasional participants on negotiating teams. The advice of special counsel is particularly important to local officials engaged in a struggle over local public resources. This advice carries some weight because it combines the specialized knowledge of the external frame of policy and judicial decisions in previous cases with the role of the trusted neutral. The special counsel is trusted because he or she is hired to represent the locality's interests exclusively; the special counsel is a neutral in that, in theory, such counsel has an objective eye and is less influenced by local considerations. Because they are experts and because they presumably have no ax to grind in the case, unlike elected and appointed local officials, special counsels often carry great weight in making decisions on whether to negotiate and on what conditions to enter negotiations.

The decision to enter and to put effort into negotiations is contingent upon local officials deciding (based on the sentiments expressed by their constituents and the advice of their special counsel) that litigation is a less desirable course of action than entering formal negotiations. This decision is only marginally influenced by the early discovery of negotiating room by each side. In most cases where ad hoc administrative and political negotiations have been abandoned and the parties have publicly moved toward impasse, the idea of offering concessions by one or both parties to initiate formal negotiations is usually rejected out of hand. Rather, the impetus toward negotiations must come from an outside source.

Negotiating Teams and Joint Sessions

In our discussion so far, we have identified negotiation subarenas on each side and several key factors and roles affecting the conduct of interlocal negotiations. We have contended that these subarenas and roles are so much a part of the overall dispute situation that the mediator must be prepared to extend his or her role so as to participate directly in the activities of the subarenas. In this session, however, we return to the major negotiation arena—the joint negotiation process that involves the two negotiating teams in joint meetings and in caucus sessions. Figure 6.2 describes the basic arrangement of two negotiating teams as they present proposals for each other's consideration through formal negotiating sessions.

Figure 6.2 indicates that each negotiating team is involved in two simultaneous processes with respect to generating proposals for exchange in the joint negotiating sessions. Each team is involved in an internal subnegotiation in which its members react to the dispute situation and generate alternative positions in efforts to achieve consensus that can be conveyed as a proposal. Simultaneously, each team engages in developing often elaborate adversarial strategies and tactics to be deployed in joint negotiation sessions. In Figure 6.2 we identify the internal negotiation decision process by which a negotiating team organizes itself as another key negotiation subarena. This subarena acts as a locus for developing proposals and considering offers to be made and offers to be accepted or rejected.

148

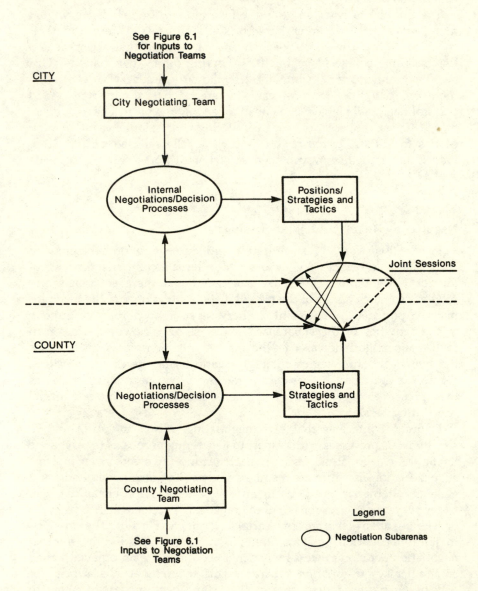

Figure 6.2
Negotiation Substructures: Joint Sessions and Caucuses

See Figure 6.1
for Inputs to
Negotiation Teams

CITY

City Negotiating Team

Internal
Negotiations/Decision
Processes

Positions/
Strategies and
Tactics

Joint Sessions

COUNTY

Internal
Negotiations/Decision
Processes

Positions/
Strategies and
Tactics

County Negotiating
Team

See Figure 6.1
Inputs to Negotiation
Teams

Legend

Negotiation Subarenas

The most easily identified negotiation setting is, of course, the joint or table negotiation session. In these settings the parties are in the same room, in turn presenting or reacting to offers and counteroffers, deploying or reacting to tactics, and, on occasion, breaking through into direct interaction and conjoint discussions.

The three negotiation subarenas in Figure 6.2 are recognizable to the parties as the joint meeting and caucus process. In the usual organization of adversarial bargaining through the middle stages of a negotiation (after which different processes take over), the parties present proposals in the joint meeting room and then have a short round of explanations and questions and answers, followed by a caucus. The subarenas are therefore spatially and temporarily separate events to the negotiators. Mediators participate in all three subarenas, adopting different roles in each. We now turn to a consideration of mediator roles in the five negotiation subarenas just identified.

Mediator Roles in Negotiation Substructures

The several negotiation subarenas previously described include three different settings in which mediators are engaged with the parties: (1) joint negotiating sessions, (2) caucus sessions with each negotiating team, and (3) meetings between negotiating teams and governing boards. Mediators may also find it useful to follow a program of planned one-to-one meetings with individual negotiators apart from group settings. In this section we review these subarenas from the viewpoint of mediator roles, activities, and objectives.

Table 6.1 summarizes four negotiation subarenas in which mediators engage the parties; in each subarena, typical mediator roles and activities are described. Except for the first subarena—joint sessions—the subarenas are found on each side of an intergovernmental dispute; thus, for example, there are two team caucuses—and a possible total of seven separate settings for mediator meetings with the parties in a two-party dispute.

Mediators are only assured access to the joint meetings of the parties. In fact, they may have only intermittent access to caucuses with one or the other party or to meetings between negotiators and their governing boards—the subarenas identified in Figure 6.2. The mediator may, for example, request to meet individually with the negotiators, to attend meetings between a negotiating team and its governing board, or, most importantly, to regularly attend caucus meetings of teams in the flow of negotiations. But access to each of these settings, or to any given meeting, depends on the willingness of the negotiators to accept the mediator in that setting.

TABLE 6.1
Mediator Roles and Activities in Negotiation Substructures

Negotiation Subarenas	Mediator Roles	Activities
Joint Sessions	Represent norms of good faith negotiation—facilitate exchange process	Draft negotiation agreements, initiate joint negotiations
		Establish negotiating formats—sequential proposals/caucuses or other formats
	Define and advoctate joint interests in the issues	Process interventions—meanings clarification
		Draft texts of joint positions
		Develop joint talking points
		Draft initial settlement agreements
		Represent process to the media
Team Caucuses	Frame issues into negotiating positions	Advice on law and policy requirements—transfer information from previous negotiation cases
	Facilitate intrateam process	Convey substantive and attitudinal information between teams
		Assist in proposal development—feedback on other team interests and requirements
		Research and draft texts—with team attorneys/consultants

		Facilitate internal position analysis
		Review joint meetings—feedback impacts of tactics/strategies
		Assist in intrateam group process—validate leadership
		Exploration of interpersonal linkages between teams which may support or disturb the negotiation
Meetings with Individual Negotiators	Develop trust relationships with the mediator	One on one meetings reviewing interests and concerns; Discuss feelings about the negotiation—about settlement as an outcome; about the dynamics of personal stakes and styles affecting the negotiation
	Surface and develop the issues	Exploration of vital interests, perspectives on the issues; ideas for reforming the issues into negotiating positions
Team Meetings with Governing Boards	Develop negotiation as an alternative to political or litigation routes	Introduce mediation role to elected officials Establish the framework for structured negotiations Advice on role composition of negotiating teams
	Represent joint session products to the governing boards; support teams	Represent and validate offers made in negotiations—a neutral perspective

Mediators in Joint Sessions

Joint negotiating sessions are always attended by the mediator. Joint sessions are used to exchange proposals, to develop shared understanding of each side's views of the crucial issues, to map the subject of the dispute into areas of unilateral concern and overlapping concern, to ensure that relevant values surface and are exchanged, and to discuss new ideas. These sessions are also used by parties to attempt to control the other side. That is, parties try to manipulate the situation to their own advantage by positioning their adversary to conform to their own negative expectations, often to justify an adversarial action. There are psycho-social dramas played out in joint sessions as adversaries seek to dominate and win the negotiation. Sparks may fly as strategies and tactics are perceived as attempts to manipulate. Interpersonal reactions to attempted manipulation will often cause hostility and anger to surface. Sometimes these feelings are openly expressed; often they surface in the form of proposals that deny the other side's interests as valid ones to be accommodated in a search for a solution. Where these dynamics prevail, the dispute cannot be settled through negotiations.

Joint sessions, then, often simultaneously include (1) concentration on the objective of the negotiation—seeking areas of compromise on the issues through a process of exchanging proposals and (2) preoccupation with the negotiators subjective perceptions of the negative aspects of adversaries' behavior—their attempt to control the negotiation by deploying manipulative strategies and tactics to gain their objectives. Mediators in joint sessions seek to support the former activities and to prevent or ameliorate the negative consequences of the latter.

Individual mediator styles are important in determining specific mediator actions in a dispute setting. Stereotypical deal-making mediators may not undertake the process interventions aimed at establishing a joint understanding of negotiation norms and a clarification of meanings. Therapist-type mediators may refuse to become involved as a go-between in the substance of the issues, that is, in making deals first with one party and then the other. In our experience in adversarial intergovernmental disputes, we find both roles essential at different stages in the negotiation.

In negotiating sessions mediators first of all represent the essential joint aspect of the negotiation, the common purpose the parties have in seeking to settle the dispute through direct talks. In many adversarial disputes, one or more of the parties see the joint settings as simply another arena for the conduct of adversarial action. That is, they seek to impose their point of view on their adversary and may have little regard for the process of compromise and problem solving. Mediators in these cases begin the negotiation by establishing a format for the negotiation that accurately addresses the parties' need to confront each other as adversaries. Yet mediators attempt to provide the process with an internal structure as a basis for shifting at a later stage in the talks to a joint process of dispute mapping and exploration of the issues and compromises. The mediator's first actions, after reconnoitering the dispute and meeting with the parties, are to establish a negotiating format for the joint sessions that fits the parties' requirements. The mediator introduces the joint nature of the negotiation and begins the long process of establishing the primacy of joint action in situations in which the parties are initially determined to pursue cautiously unilateral action.

Mediators often begin their advocacy of the joint process by sealing off the negotiators from outside influences, adopting a special neutral setting and regular time for the talks, and isolating the negotiators from the media. They may introduce the idea of a negotiation agreement in which the parties bind themselves not to make independent statements to the press and not to use the products of the negotiation in any other setting—for example, offers made in negotiation are not to be used in court or in public. In a second strategy, in cases where parties have a history of interlocal conflict and suspicion of each other's motives and tactics, mediators frequently open a discussion on the meaning of good faith negotiations in the particular dispute context. They monitor this discussion and may contribute to it with the purpose of reinforcing the parties' sense of the mediator as the representative of the norms of good faith negotiation. Mediators cannot, of course, impose a standard for negotiations on parties, but often the discussion itself establishes these norms and surfaces perceived past injustices that the parties do not want repeated in the negotiation. The parties thus are encouraged to surface some of the standards they intend to use to judge each other's statements and actions in the negotiations.

The mediator may also engage the parties in conversations about the way negotiations ought to be conducted—for example, topics of such conversations include negotiation formats, timing, and team composition. Through these discussions of the process they intend to follow, disputing parties are drawn into their first action: the fashioning of agreements over the rules of the negotiation. The mediator, symbolically representing the parties' joint interests, plays an important role in these discussions by representing norms of good faith negotiation as the parties' mutually define these norms in the informal ground rules they may establish.

In most cass the negotiation format is one of joint meetings with caucuses intermingled at the mediator's or the parties' discretion. This model supports both joint discussion of positions and separate discussion, for limited periods, by each side. It addresses the need for joint contact and the need for separation and discussion among team members (the latter to serve as a release from the pressures that can be built up in the joint sessions). The format usually is cast as a sequence of formal proposals made alternatively by each side. The idea is to establish a norm of reciprocity; proposals and counterproposals are exchanged sequentially by the parties in joint session. In practice, formal proposals are usually written and are accompanied by the settlement vehicle of a presentation that extols its virtues. The side receiving the proposal then usually asks questions to clarify their understanding of the presenting team's points and vital interests. Not infrequently these questions uncover the receiving team's rejection of the proposal and its premises. After a brief question period, the receiving team typically calls a caucus to review the proposal in private and to decide on a response during that negotiating session. Often they will return to the joint session only briefly, then request the negotiation to adjourn to a new session when they will formally present a counterproposal.

Having established the proposal-counterproposal process as the main format through the early stages in the negotiation, the mediator monitors its implementation and intervenes selectively to maintain the process. The mediator may choose to simply chair the meetings in which proposal exchanges are going on, allowing the parties to define the issues through their proposals and to confront one another on issues and feelings. Mediator interventions may well be limited at this point to the clarification of meanings communicated and to the enforcement of the norms of the negotiation as earlier discussed by the parties and the mediator.

If the parties are able to move closer together by using the sequence of proposals and counterproposals, they will be slowly building a commitment to the negotiation process. However well they proceed in this process, almost inevitably an impasse will be reached that serves the parties' requirements for adversarial contact. These impasses may quickly cause the breakdown of the negotiation. At an impasse the mediator may become much more active by involving him or herself directly in the issues. The mediator may call for caucuses or suspend a joint meeting in order to review the issues of the impasse with each team separately. Then the mediator must decide on an approach toward the impasse: if it should be confronted by reframing it in a different context or by finding acceptable tradeoffs from one side to the other or by simply asking the parties to defer further discussion of the issue, putting it off until other aspects of the dispute are settled. Mediators emerge at the point of impasse from their relatively passive role to their active role. In the face of an impasse threatening the negotiation, they may move on their own initiative to find a path to maintaining the negotiation. They must combine a sense of timing with a deep involvement in the substance of the impasse issues to bring forward a way to keep the negotiations alive.

After meeting separately with the negotiating teams and sometimes individually with certain key negotiators, mediators may draft a text or a written set of negotiating points and work with these from side to side, finding mutual adjustments and continually reworking these points until the overall path to resolving the impasse is on paper. The mediators may continue this process until settlement terms are reached or, having resolved a specific impasse, they may rely once again on the parties' direct interactions in joint meetings. They may, that is, retreat from a high profile in the dispute and move back to the role of monitor of the parties' interactions in joint negotiating sessions.

The essential mediator role in joint sessions is as the advocate of the parties' joint interests: first in the issues and second in the process exchange. An adversarial atmosphere usually is present at the initiation of the joint sessions and throughout most of the joint meetings. The experienced mediator will not attempt to move the parties away from the adversarial process faster than they are willing to move themselves. Rather, mediators define and support a way of conducting an adversarial negotiation process through which the parties can learn about each other's interests and requirements. The mediation theory underlying this approach to negotiations relies on the parties' own development of the negotiations fueled by their increasing investment in the joint outcomes. This approach presumes that when the parties are ready, they will move away from the adversarial process to joint exploration of the issues and the means for compromise to settlement. The mediators act to sustain the negotiations until joint action emerges by working with the issues, cutting deals to maintain the negotiation and move it forward, and by working with the parties' feelings about the negotiation and about one another's actions.

Mediators in Caucus Meetings

In this discussion we use the term "caucus" to refer to the side meetings of negotiating teams apart from the joint negotiating sessions. Caucuses are used to develop and refine negotiating positions before joint meetings, to process individual reactions to events in preceding joint meetings, and to recapitulate in previous negotiating sessions, reviewing the session and developing strategies for upcoming sessions.

In caucuses, freed from the social requirements of the joint setting, negotiators' reactions to the adversarial experience are allowed free rein. Without the pressure of having the other side across the table, negotiators are free to characterize their adversaries' motives in ways that best support their personal views of the dispute. In many instances caucuses begin with castigations of the other negotiators' motives, motives often perceived as seeking to act totally against a reasonable negotiation, as acting in bad faith, and as attempting to manipulate the situation to their own advantage. In the early confrontational stages of a negotiation, a team member who in caucus speaks positively about actions of the other side in joint sessions may be seen as soft by the other team members and may lose credibility within the team.

There is much projection in caucuses. In these side meetings negotiators may give voice to their feelings of frustration at being blocked and at having proposals rejected in the joint session. In the early stages of a negotiation, the caucus often develops into a chorus of reinforcing deprecations of the value of the negotiation itself. Team members verbalize that their own approach to the negotiation is both a rational furthering of their interests and conciliatory. They may insist to one another and to the mediator that they are open, that their proposals are indeed fair— that they are the good guys. They are usually unwilling to ascribe any of these virtues to the other team as a whole.

Intrateam Dynamics. Negotiating teams in interjurisdictional disputes are composed of elected officials, who may represent differing constituencies, and a few senior public administrators. They form a small group, and in the way of small groups to accomplish any goal they must first organize themselves internally—they must select a mode of operation and they must develop leader roles, supporting roles, and ways of processing information and arriving at decisions. Typically negotiating teams observe these group process requirements by specifying a spokesperson for the group and by developing an understanding of consensual decisionmaking in which appointed officials defer to elected officials in all activities except for perhaps position development activities. These natural sortings of internal organization roles may be sufficient to effectively manage the negotiating team in the dispute, but they may not be.

The socio-psychological dynamics of the adversarial negotiation encourage polarization when parties move from the joint setting to the caucus. We previously described some of the attitudinal breaks in the negotiation that naturally surface in caucuses—that is, the verbalization of feelings and frustration expressed as the confrontation between the good guys (us) and the bad guys (them). To a certain degree this unrealistic polarization serves natural processes of group identification and integration in the face of adversaries. It is much easier, after all, for a group to act in a concerted manner if the adversary is hostile and plainly can't be trusted to negotiate openly. If the group agrees that the adversary's proposals are ridiculous and that the adversary is not acting in good faith, then the group can easily function as a cohesive unit. The problem, of course, is that the counteraction by a party that finds its adversary's proposals ridiculous and that its adversary acted in bad faith is to put forward only very narrow counterproposals and to develop tactics calculated to manipulate the other side.

When negotiating teams face proposals they consider to be unacceptable offers and when they receive personally slighting remarks, they are obviously more likely to move away from the negotiation than toward it. In such settings the leadership role in the group may demand turning the group back to the substance of issues and to consideration of the alternatives to a negotiated settlement. In particular, leaders interested in settlement must move team members away from defensive positioning and punitive actions by focusing on tactics developed to move the negotiation forward rather than on tactics to protect existing positions or to punish the other side for not responding in good faith to proposals previously offered. In situations requiring such guidance, leaders often emerge. Clearly they have a difficult role to play. To an important extent success in the negotiation depends on the abilities of the group's leaders to get team members to explore the issues and alternatives rather than to configure negotiating positions as retaliations for unacceptable offers made by their adversaries.

Mediators in caucuses, as in joint sessions, have a dual purpose: to promote parties' consideration of the substantive issues and the possibilities for new formulations, tradeoffs, and compromises and to assist the parties to overcome problems they encounter with the internal dynamics of their negotiating team—the internal group processes employed for the consideration of issues and development of negotiating positions.

We have outlined a common scenario of a team caucus through the beginnings and middle stages of an adversarial interjurisdictional negotiation. In our experience, the development of the negotiating team as a social group capable of action in the face of the pressures of the adversarial setting is a key to successful negotiations. Thus we believe that the events in the caucus setting, in which positions are developed to be put forward in joint settings, is absolutely as important as the events of the joint setting to the outcome of the negotiations.

As we have indicated there are negative pressures on a newly formed negotiating team that move the group toward a consensus of rejection of positive negotiation. Through the internal dynamics of the group and the actions of the group's leaders these negative pressures may be challenged to move the group to positive action. In this way, the internal dynamics of the group and the group leaders are the primary determinants of the future of the negotiations.

Mediators inside caucuses can assist team leaders in their discussion of the situation and their attempts to formulate group policy. On one level, mediators assist the group by supporting development of the leadership role in action—namely, by reinforcing the leader's statements, by facilitating internal discussions on the issues, and by working through statements by group members about the internal processes of the negotiating team. In most teams there are what Thomas Colosi has called nonstabilizers—individuals whose objective is to disrupt the team's attempt to negotiate, to have the team quit the negotiation and pursue other means. If the leader and others influential in the group support continued negotiations, the mediator works to develop the primacy of the group consensus and to reduce the effects of nonstabilizers on the group consideration of the issues.[1]

This description of negotiators' reactions to the talks in caucus and of the internal processes of small groups necessary to move toward positive group action has not yet included any specification of the mediator's involvement in the substantive issues with the parties in caucus. It is to this involvement by the mediator in the primary issues of the dispute that we now turn.

Mediator Involvement in the Issues. As previously stated, the caucus serves negotiators as the setting for initially developing negotiating positions and for reformulating positions. At different points in a dispute, mediators often separate the parties and shuttle back and forth between them with information and position reformulations. By this action the mediator takes central stage in the caucus in the presentation of positions and in their interpretation. Often a team will develop a written position and ask the mediator to transmit it and get a response, having predetermined their own alternative responses. These attempts to control the negotiation are undertaken primarily as self-protective measures.

Encountering such a strategy, mediators may in caucus attempt to turn the situation back on the team formulating the position, asking how they would react to such a strategy deployed against themselves. The mediators seek, and may demand, a wider range of alternatives, all of which cannot have ready responses. In making these requests mediators are looking to avoid premature closure by providing feedback to parties regarding the probable effects of their strategies to unilaterally determine the options available in offers.

In the process of conveying written or verbal offers from one side to another in caucuses, mediators are regularly asked by the team they are meeting with about the intent of the other side, the degree of their seriousness, and the specifics of the offer. Mediators are often questioned closely, intently, about the other side's attitudes; mediators attempt to feedback accurate information if parties have not instructed them to limit their comments on intentions toward future positions on issues. Part of the close questioning of the mediator may be an effort by nonstabilizers in negotiations to find out the mediator's allegiances and to position the mediator as the ally of the other side and an untrustworthy partner in the negotiations. At the same time, the investigation by the team of the other team's involvement in the issues and of their willingness to make further compromises than they have already put on the table is most important to the stabilizers in the negotiation in their effort to reach beyond the purely adversarial context to mutual accommodation and settlement. Thus the discussion in caucus of the attitudes of one side and the future of the negotiation is a critical element in the position reformulating process.

At the point of reformulating past offers, mediators support the group's leaders by providing skills in managing meetings (facilitation toward a group product) or in applied writing (drafting position statements and texts), that is if the group needs such assistance. If the group does not require assistance—if it includes skilled meeting managers or text drafters— the mediator may elect to be on the sidelines, encouraging the group's own development of its product.

By virtue of their involvement in a specific class of disputes, mediators gain specialized knowledge of the substantive issues in the dispute and of the details of negotiated settlements of adjudication in other, similar cases. In the case of interjurisdictional disputes regulated by another level of government (state or federal agencies), mediators may have access to the regulating agency's executives or they may be seen by the disputants as the representative of that agency. Thus, apart from their self-described role as neutrals, mediators may be seen as experts in the subject matter and even as sources of authority on the issues, as long as the mediator's suggestions do not violate the parties' views of their own interests. Mediator's association with the regulating agency and, at the point of action, the mediator's personal knowledge of alternative settlement patterns often are useful to the negotiators when they are stuck on the issues of a counterproposal. The mediator may, for example, review with the parties the likely outcome of a court-ordered settlement, based on his or her knowledge of other cases, as one option (for example, quitting the negotiation), then request the negotiators to weigh that option against offers on the table and to consider what is possible to achieve by continuing the negotiations. Thus, mediators may become deeply involved in the parties' consideration of their alternatives in deciding on new negotiating positions.

Furthermore, mediators may on their own initiative put forward proposal alternatives that they feel may be acceptable to the other side to test them, to look for acceptance. In many cases such proposals will be rejected because they go too far at the time. The mediator may respond by suggesting that the proposal be conveyed not as a counterproposal but as a mediator proposal. If acceptance is found, then the mediator may come back requesting that the initiating team formally put forward the proposal. Thus, the mediator may work at the interstices of the issues, trying to separate the substance from the emotionally laden aspect of parties seeing proposals as demands.

Occasionally when parties are at an impasse, mediators in caucus stimulate discussion of wide-ranging reformulations of whole positions, adopting new reference frames and thus new premises for the parties' consideration. For example, in Virginia in several boundary disputes, after reaching an impasse in negotiations over new boundary lines, parties have at the mediator's suggestion moved to discuss variations of joint revenue-sharing or consolidation of public services as a complement to municipal annexation. In these instances mediators may take responsibility for doing technical staff work on the new positions until the parties see something promising in the proposal and are willing to invest their own effort in it. In several cases such proposals have blossomed into a contract between the adversaries to hire an outside consulting firm to develop a joint study for the negotiators. The contract required the development of a single database for use by both parties, as well as the development of alternatives specifying different ways of resolving the dispute. At the point of developing the contract requirements and hiring the consultant, the negotiators clearly had moved to a new, nonadversarial stage in the negotiation. (In one case a return to adversarial positioning awaited the completion of the joint study however.) In these cases an explicit articulation of the evolutionary phases of the dispute was particularly evident. Different mediator roles were called for at different stages in the dispute.

Other Mediator Meetings and Roles

There are two other settings or subarenas in an intergovernmental negotiation in which mediators, acting either on their own initiative or at the negotiator's request, may further the development of a negotiated settlement. First are the mediator's meetings with individual members of negotiating teams held apart from their meetings with the team as a whole. Second are the meetings in which negotiating teams brief their primary constituents—the governing boards—on settlement terms and processes; in these meetings the mediator's role is the neutral representative of settlement.

In our earlier discussion of team caucuses we placed considerable emphasis on the social nature of the negotiation process within negotiating teams as well as in the dynamics of the joint sessions. It is hard to overstate the hidden influence of social group processes within negotiating teams in controlling the output of those teams—the content of their proposals in the negotiation. And sometimes when dysfunctional interpersonal dynamics disturb the smooth functioning of the negotiating team—like the disruption if an individual dominates other team members or if there are opposing political camps within a team that tend to cancel each other out and leave the team immobilized—mediators may find it important to mediate within the team.

Mediators cannot assume that negotiating teams will operate as cohesive, well-integrated units that make decisions by consensus. As suggested above, such assumptions may ignore turbulence within a negotiating team, which may be tantamount to giving up prematurely on the negotiation, where, for example, there are interpersonal or political differences among team members that are not addressed. The only consensus position achievable among team members under pressure to respond to proposals may be the devaluation of the negotiation and the willingness to abandon it for other options.

To avoid premature closure in negotiations, mediators can adopt quasi-mediation roles within negotiating teams. The role is not fully developed because it is temporary and very targeted, defined by particular issues and problems; mediators in this role have an immediate goal of providing a resolution of the given problem (that is, development of a negotiating position). The role is not imposed nor formally discussed as a role. Rather, the mediator may simply act—namely, by meeting separately with individual members of the negotiating team, focusing on the discussion of strategy for the joint negotiation, and attempting in separate meetings with the negotiators to pull together a negotiating position that can be affirmed as the team position in a team meeting. Should the individual members question the mediator's actions within the team, the mediator describes precisely his or her purpose in the side meetings and expresses the willingness to abandon the effort at a word from the parties. Despite its apparent risks, this procedure has been useful to negotiating teams at particular points within the course of a long negotiation.

There are two other reasons for separate meetings between mediators and individual members of negotiating teams. One is to establish a level of personal contact between negotiators and mediators. The other is to enable the mediator to gain insights into the dispute and the local settlement options from people who have long experience in the particular locale, who possess a memory of the intergovernmental scene that may condition the range of acceptable settlement options. Again, we observe here the two themes of the mediator role: (1) the effort to establish the interpersonal contact, trusting relations, and understanding necessary for the parties to agree to any course of action and (2) the search for facts and the debate over courses of action that may lead to settlement.

Mediators' meetings with the negotiating teams as a whole are focused on the overall negotiation, on what the other team is doing. Meetings with individual members of a negotiating team allow time for the mediator to establish a relationship with the negotiators; the meetings allow for an individual response to their personal requirements. The one-to-one meetings also enable the mediator to review positions at length with the individual negotiators, allowing them to voice their special concerns that may not get expressed in the joint setting. In addition, the mediator can become aware of individual negotiators' views of the issues and ideas for settlement. In several cases, these one-to-one meetings have provided the critical information from which settlement conditions eventually emerged. These meetings complement meetings with the full negotiating team, reaching beyond what the team as a whole communicates.

A final subarena for mediator participation in negotiations involves assisting negotiating teams in dealing with their governing boards. This role is evident at the beginning of negotiations, when teams are first appointed and the mediation process is explained to the local governments, and often again at the end of negotiations. At the initiation of negotiations, elected officials have numerous questions about the unfamiliar negotiation process they are embarking on, about the mediator's experience and bias, and about the negotiation process itself. The mediator, by explaining negotiation processes used in other communities and in other disputes, lays out the framework for the negotiation and introduces the mediation role to the elected officials. The mediator may give advice to the parties on the composition of negotiating teams and may explain the role of the negotiation in the context of other paths to dispute resolution. These basic discussions are nearly always necessary because usually the governing boards have had no prior experience with mediators in structured policy negotiations. Occasionally, at either midway through or at the end of negotiations, mediators are requested to make presentations to local governing boards. Negotiating teams also sometimes find it useful to have the mediator describe the process of the negotiation and to validate the scope of offers, the concessions made by the other side, and the shape of the overall settlement. Mediators only engage governing boards in discussions of the negotiations at the explicit request of the negotiating teams.

Notes

Introduction

1. See Chapter 2 of this book for a review of the statutory background of Virginia's municipal annexation process.

2. This vignette is actually the combination of two disputes, which occurred one year and a hundred miles apart. The county officials under pressure in each negotiation used almost identical words. The prevalence of civil war battlefields in Virginia is well known. Locally historic battles had been fought in the area of each dispute, and weapons were available.

3. For a more general review of Virginia's mediation program, see Roger Richman, "Formal Mediation in Intergovernmental Disputes: Virginia Municipal Annexation Negotiations in Virginia," *Public Administration Review* 45, no. 4 (July/August 1985):510–517.

4. Most cases in environmental mediation (currently the most prominent subfield of public policy mediation) have been mediated by a few established centers around the country. Within these centers the mediators share experiences in refining their models of appropriate instances in which an administrative agency regulating a dispute arena has supported the use of mediation in a series of similar cases, cases in which the disputants change but the issues and the statutes regulating the dispute are constant. The Mediation Institute in Seattle had such a program with the Federal Regional Council several years ago, and, more recently, the New England Environmental Mediation Center had referred to it a stream of estuarine management cases for negotiations by the state's coastal conservation agencies. More substantive, in 1981 and 1983 Massachusetts and Wisconsin, respectively, adopted statutes structuring the use of mediation procedures in solid and hazardous waste site selection processes.

5. This scorecard, seven negotiated settlements from fourteen cases with three cases currently in negotiations, represents the mediation caseload from November 1980 (the Commission on Local Government's first case) to September 1985. In four cases mediation processes have broken down and the parties proceeded to litigation to settle their dispute. Classification of the caseload into settled and litigated cases is not always clear cut. In certain cases negotiated settlements have later been abandoned. In other cases, listed as nonsettled, litigation was halted after the parties did reach a negotiated settlement. We have listed as settled cases those where mediator led negotiations resulted in a written agreement signed by the parties and submitted to a state agency or court for external review.

Chapter 1

1. One could, of course, reject this proposition and claim as a theory of action that mediators ought to impose their own conditions on the dispute and dominate the negotiation, presumably since they are in a position to disregard the vagaries of the parties' noncognitive experiences and expeditiously to pursue settlement conditions. This model is, we feel, inappropriate and dysfunctional as a means of settling complex public disputes in which the parties are engaged in ongoing relations and in which implementation of settlement is contingent upon joint action.

2. This section draws from the ideas developed in Donald A. Schon, *The Reflective Practitioner* (New York: Basic Books, 1983).

Chapter 2

1. There appears to be no clear explanation as to how or why Virginia developed the independent city system. The system evolved slowly and unobtrusively through the years. See Chester W. Bain, *A Body Incorporate: The Evolution of City-County Separation in Virginia* (Charlottesville, Va.: University Press of Virginia, 1967).

2. See Code of Virginia, 1950, Secs. 15.1–982.1 through 15.1–982.8 hereafter cited in text and notes as Va. Code. The process by which towns in Virginia may become cities was made much more lengthy and difficult as a result of legislation adopted in 1979. The process now requires a vote by town residents, review by the new Commission on Local Government, and ultimately approval by the court. Prior to the 1979 change in the law a town could become an independent city merely by action of its governing body and determination by the court that the town had a population of at least 5,000 persons.

3. Town annexations do not remove any property (including real, personal, machinery, and tools) from the county's tax rolls and thus do not constrict any county property taxes. Town annexations do reduce a county's sales tax receipts, vehicle license taxes, and other minor revenues.

4. Towns in Virginia are not required to become cities when they attain a population of 5,000 persons. As of 1980 Virginia had fourteen towns with population that exceeded that figure. The largest town in Virginia is Blacksburg, whose 1980 population (30,638) constituted 48.2 percent of that of its parent county.

5. Five basic processes are used throughout the nation for the resolution of annexation issues—popular determination (referendum), unilateral municipal action, judicial review, special act of the state legislature, and review by an expert administrative body.

6. The criteria for the determination of annexation issues now include the need of the municipality to increase its tax base and to obtain additional land for development, the urban service needs of the area proposed for annexation and the capacity of the municipality to meet those needs, the community of interest between the annexing municipality and the area proposed for annexation,

and the adverse effect on the county of the proposed annexation. See Va. Code, Sec. 15.1–1041.

7. *Henrico County* v. *City of Richmond,* 106 Va. 282 (1904).

8. See *Report of the Commission on City-County Relationships,* House Document No. 27, 1975 General Assembly Session, Appendix G. No comprehensive tabulation of town annexations in Virginia has ever been made.

9. The major studies undertaken were those by the Commission to Study Urban Growth (1950), the Virginia Advisory Legislative Council (1962), the Virginia Metropolitan Areas Study Commission (1966), the Commission to Study Problems of the Expansion of the Boundaries of Richmond (1969), the Commission on City-County Relationships (1975), and the Commission on State Aid to Localities (1978).

10. The variance in population profiles, or the emerging development of such, has been seen as a factor prompting municipal annexation as well. See John V. Moeser and Rutledge M. Dennis, *The Politics of Annexation: Oligarchic Power in a Southern City* (Cambridge, Mass.: Schentman Publishing, 1982).

11. The cost of a contested annexation case in Virginia can be extraordinary, even approaching or exceeding $1 million for a single party. See *Report of the Commission on City-County Relationships* (1975), pp. 77–78.

12. The vehemency over some annexation issues in Virginia may be hard to overstate. The intensity of feeling is reflected in a statement made to the author by a legislator representing a county affected by a recent annexation. The legislator remarked that he had included a provision in his will that prohibited his body from being interred by a funeral establishment owned by the family of the mayor of the city that had annexed his residence.

13. *Report of the Commission on City-County Relationships,* p. 9. (Hereafter when material from this report is quoted in the text, applicable page numbers will appear in parentheses following the quotation.)

14. The immunity proposed by the commission would not have prohibited either annexations by towns or annexations to cities initiated by petititon of county residents or property owners. The former annexations would not threaten the territorial integrity of the county (given the proposed prohibition against the establishment of new cities within immune counties) and the latter type of annexation has tended to be modest in scope and impact.

15. This recommendation led to the subsequent establishment of a Commission on State Aid to Localities, which addressed the plight of core cities and the equity of state aid programs.

16. Under previous law the courts had been given only a limited, ministerial role in new city incorporations. For example, in town-to-city transitions the courts were only required to ascertain that the town had a population of 5,000 or more prior to its entering an order establishing city status. Prior to the change in law resulting from the commission's recommendations, counties in Virginia could obtain city status only by special act of the legislature.

17. The General Assembly did not consider the commission's proposals during the 1975 legislative session because of the breadth and complexity of the proposals. The 1976 session of the General Assembly established a joint committee

composed of members of both houses of the legislature to examine in detail the commission's recommendations.

18. The companion measure was HB2160. This bill would have established a new state funding formula for general use in the distribution of state aid and would have directed substantially increased state assistance to localities for which specified statistical indices revealed low fiscal ability, high tax effort, and general need. See M. H. Wilkinson, "The Commission on State Aid to Localities: The Search for Equity in State Assistance," *Virginia Town and City*, November 1977.

19. The economic growth-sharing provisions in HB855 called for each participating locality (the city and all adjoining immunized counties) to contribute to the revenue pool a sum equal to (1) 40 percent of the increase in the value of its taxable industrial and commercial property (based on growth above a base year) multiplied by the lowest real property tax rate used by any participating locality and (2) 40 percent of its growth in local sales tax receipts. Disbursements from the pool were to be based upon each locality's population adjusted by its relative fiscal ability, tax effort, and need.

20. Virtually every session of the General Assembly in recent decades has seen the introduction of bills calling for annexations to be determined by referendum; and the state's municipalities were concerned that some future session of the legislature might enact such a measure. Fear of such a possibility could well have prompted a deluge of annexation activity.

21. George R. Long, Executive Director, Virginia Association of Counties, "Report of the Executive Director, 1976–1977" (mimeographed), November 14, 1977.

22. "Statement by the Virginia Municipal League and the Virginia Association of Counties to House Committee on Counties, Cities and Towns," February 7, 1978. (Hereafter when material from this statement is quoted in the text, applicable page numbers will appear in parentheses following the quotation.)

23. Although the original concept of permitting the state's most heavily and densely populated counties to obtain immunity for their entire territory would remain in the legislation, this new concept of partial immunity would apply to all the commonwealth's counties.

24. As this provision was to evolve, a grant of partial immunity to a county would rest principally upon a determination that (1) the area was receiving appropriate urban-type services of a scope and quality comparable to that provided in the adjoining city, (2) the county had made appropriate efforts to comply with state policies regarding education, housing, public transportation, planning, and other issues, and (3) the community of interest between the area for which immunity was sought and the county generally exceeded that which existed between the area and the adjoining city. The factors governing the disposition of partial immunity actions are now codified in Va. Code, Sec. 15.1–977.22:1.

25. The chief patron of HB603 was Thomas J. Michie, Jr., then a delegate, who had been a member of the Commission on City-County Relationships and who from the beginning had led the legislative effort to revise the state's

annexation and transition law. Michie's skilled, resourceful, and tireless leadership was primarily responsible for the new legislation under which the state's localities now function.

26. A clause in HB603 required the enactment and funding of companion legislation (HB599) designed to increase state aid to localities as a precondition for the termination of the various moratoriums and for the implementation of the new immunity provisions. Thomas J. Michie, Jr., was the chief patron of HB599.

27. Va. Code, Sec. 15.1–945.1. The original appointees had had experience in national, state, and local governmental activities as well as service in all types of Virginia's political subdivisions. By vocation, the original appointees were engineers, lawyers, public administrators, and businessmen. Collectively, the five original appointees had over a century of service in Virginia local government.

28. Va. Code, Sec. 15.1–945.7(A). The commission has no role in reviewing petitions by counties for total immunity. The court's role in the review of total immunity actions is limited merely to ascertaining whether the county seeking immunity has the requisite population and population density required by law for such immunization. As finally enacted, HB603 permitted any county having a population of 20,000 and a population density of 300 persons per square mile or any county having a population of 50,000 and a population density of 140 persons per square mile to seek and obtain a grant of total immunity. Although these criteria appear to be quite low, less than ten of Virginia's ninety-five counties met the population standards for total immunity.

29. Va. Code, Sec. 15.1–945.7(A). Negotiations under the commission's auspices may be held in executive session.

30. Negotiations under this provision of law cannot extend beyond one year unless the parties agree otherwise.

31. The mediators initially identified for service under the commission's auspices had backgrounds principally in the fields of public administration, political science, and planning. Each of the prospective mediators had previously been engaged in some form of conflict resolution work.

32. Commission on Local Government, "Addendum Proposal," 1982-1984 Biennial Budget.

33. The City of Harrisonburg had originally filed its petititon for annexation with a special annexation court in May 1975, but the court's consideration of the petititon was stayed by the moratorium imposed by the General Assembly. When the moratorium was ended in July 1980, the court referred the issue to the commission for review pursuant to the new legislation. All subsequent cases have been submitted to the Commission on Local Government for review, in accordance with the new statutory requirement, prior to their presentation to the court.

34. Neither the city nor the county invoked the newly authorized mandatory negotiations process.

35. Normally the commission schedules its formal hearings on an issue approximately sixty to seventy-five days after its receipt of notice of a proposed action.

36. Members of the commission and its staff have met intermittently with local government officials and with negotiating parties to provide technical information and, in a few instances, to encourage the continuance of negotiations that appeared to have reached an impasse.

37. See *County of Rockingham* v. *City of Harrisonburg*, 224, Va. 62 (1982).

38. The three other jurisdictions were the City of Covington, the City of Clifton Forge, and the Town of Iron Gate.

39. Although the Commission on Local Government has never requested an official opinion from the Office of the Attorney General on the issue, that office has advised the commission informally that a commission-designated mediator carries with him the same exemption from the State's Freedom of Information Act as the agency itself has been granted. Under this construction of the law, a commission-designated mediator may conduct negotiations with local officials in executive session.

40. This action filed by Spotsylvania County was the first instance in which a Virginia county had sought to use the state's new partial immunity statute.

41. Since the negotiations between the city and county resulted in a proposed boundary expansion by Fredericksburg conditioned on the city's agreement not to institute any further annexation attempts affecting Spotsylvania County for a twenty-five-year period, the issue formally before the commission was an annexation accompanied by a long-term self-imposed moratorium.

42. A copy of the agreement is set forth as Appendix A in Commission on Local Government, *Report on the City of Fredericksburg–County of Spotsylvania Annexation and Immunity Agreement*, June 1982. The agreement contained provisions that required the city to decline any resident-initiated annexation unless the county agreed to the boundary change. The agreement also contained a provision extending the life of the accord beyond the twenty-five-year period if certain conditions prevailed.

43. The trial court's order endorsed the proposed annexation but avoided incorporating into its terms the twenty-five-year moratorium.

44. A copy of this agreement is set forth as Appendix A in Commission on Local Government, *Report on the Town of Leesburg–County of Loudoun Annexation Agreement*, March 1983. The commission did not express any reservations about the lengthy moratoriums contained in this agreement because the net effect of the moratoriums was to protect the options of both localities and to maintain the status quo ante.

45. Although Virginia remains a Dillon Rule state, it has for decades been very permissive in allowing local governments to fashion their own distinct relations with neighboring units of local government. The General Assembly's generous grants of authority to the state's local governments prompted the Virginia Municipal League and the Virginia Association of Counties to oppose a proposal to have the Dillon Rule expressly reversed in the state's new constitution adopted in 1970. The local government associations feared that a reversal of Dillon's Rule might result in a decrease in local prerogatives. See M. H. Wilkinson and Clifton McCleskey, "Virginia," in Stephanie Cole, ed., *Partnership Within the States: Local Self-government in the Federal System* (Institute of Government

and Public Affairs, University of Illinois and Center for the Study of Federalism, Temple University, 1976), pp. 293–302.

46. Not all these eighteen interlocal settlements have been implemented. As of May 1, 1985, four of them were awaiting commission review. Six of the interjurisdictional settlements were negotiated directly by the parties without any mediation assistance being provided by the commission.

47. Prior to the enactment of the new mediation and negotiation processes there were several interlocal agreements relating to boundary change and transition issues. Those agreements, however, were qualitatively different from those adopted since 1980.

Chapter 3

1. Town and county population estimates from 1980 census adjusted by local analysis to 1982, the year of the negotiation. Rapid growth in these communities since 1982 has dated these figures.

2. *Leesburg Area Management Plan*, County of Loudoun, Va., Office of County Planning, Leesburg, Va., 1982.

3. Town of Leesburg, Negotiation, Negotiation Documents, 1982, unpublished.

Chapter 4

1. This case presents a composite of issues (revenue sharing, annexation, immunity from annexation) found in several different boundary disputes in Virginia. The case setting, negotiation processes, and mediator interventions are accurately described, the negotiating positions and statements of the parties put forward in the case are a synthesis of positions taken by parties in a number of the twelve annexation cases negotiated by the authors, and should not be attributed to parties in any one case.

2. Annexation-immunity refers to the statutory procedures in Virginia by which municipalities seek to annex land and by which counties seek to have land declared immune from annexation. Chapter 2 reviews these concepts as the legal basis of Virginia's boundary adjustments process.

3. The indicated size of the county and the city, and future references to the size of proposed annexation or immunity areas, have been altered to prevent identification of the actual communities involved in this case.

4. The indicated dates and all subsequent dates and years cited in the case have been altered to prevent identification of the parties in the case. The sequence of dates relative to one another however, remains as it was in the real-world events described in the case.

The emergence of new state legislation in the midst of the agreement seeking stage of this case was a specific event that directly affected the course of this case.

Chapter 5

1. The following selected readings in sociology, psychology, and negotiation theory and practice provide the conceptual underpinnings for some of the ideas put forward in this chapter.

Archibald, K. A. "Three Views of the Experts Role in Policy Making." *Policy Sciences* (1970), pp. 73–86.

Garfinkel, Harold. *Studies in Ethnomethodology.* Englewood Cliffs, N.J.: Prentice-Hall, 1967.

Johnston, Roger W. "Negotiation Strategies: Different Strokes for Different Folks." *Personnel* (1982), pp. 36–44.

Laing, R. D., H. Phillipson, and A. R. Lee. *Interpersonal Perception.* London: Tavistock Publications, 1966.

Morely, Ian, and Geoffrey Stephenson. *The Social Psychology of Bargaining.* London: Allen & Unwin.

Schein, Edgar. *Process Consultation.* Reading, Mass.: Addison-Wesley, 1969.

Zartman, I. William, and Maureen Berman. *The Practical Negotiator.* New Haven: Yale University Press, 1982.

Chapter 6

1. Thomas Colosi, "Negotiations in the Public and Private Sectors: A Core Mode." *American Behavioral Scientist* 27 (Nov. 1983):1.

Bibliography

Books

Abel, Richard, ed. *The Politics of Informal Justice*. The American Experience, vol. I. New York: Academic Press, 1982.

Auerback, Jerold S. *Justice Without Law*. New York: Oxford University Press, 1983.

Bacharach, S. B., and E. J. Lawler. *Bargaining Power, Tactics, and Outcomes*. San Francisco: Jossey-Bass, 1980.

Bacow, Lawrence, and Michael Wheeler. *Environmental Dispute Resolution*. New York: Plenum, 1983.

Bain, Chester W. *Annexation in Virginia*. Charlottesville: University of Virginia Press, 1966.

———. *"A Body Incorporate": The Evolution of City-County Consolidation in Virginia*. Charlottesville: University of Virginia Press, 1967.

Bazerman, Max, and Roy Lewicki, eds. *Negotiating in Organizations*. Beverly Hills: Sage, 1983.

Bingham, Gail. *Resolving Environmental Disputes: A Decade of Experience*. Washington, D.C.: The Conservation Foundation, 1985.

Dunlop, John. *Dispute Resolution: Negotiation and Consensus Building*. Dover, Mass.: Auburn House, 1984.

Fisher, Roger, and William Ury. *Getting to Yes: Negotiating Agreement Without Giving In*. Boston: Houghton Mifflin, 1981.

Garfinkel, Harold. *Studies in Ethnomethodology*. Englewood Cliffs, N.J.: Prentice-Hall, 1967.

Huelsburg, Nancy, and William Lincoln, eds. *Successful Negotiating in Local Government*. Washington, D.C.: International City Management Association, 1985.

Keirsey, David, and Marilyn Bates. *Please Understand Me*. Del Mar, Ca.: Prometheus Nemesis, 1978.

Laing, R. D., H. Phillipson, and A. R. Lee. *Interpersonal Perception*. London: Tavistock Publications, 1966.

Moeser, John V., and Dennis M. Rutledge. *The Politics of Annexation: Oligarchic Power in a Southern City*. Cambridge, Mass.: Schentman Publishing Co., 1982.

Morely, Ian, and Geoffrey Stephenson. *The Social Psychology of Bargaining*. London: Allan & Unwin.

Pruitt, Dean. *Negotiation Behavior*. New York: Academic Press, 1981.

Raiffa, H. *The Act and Science of Negotiation*. Cambridge, Mass.: Harvard University Press, 1982.

Rubin, Jeffery and Bert Brown. *The Social Psychology of Bargaining and Negotiation.* New York: Academic Press, 1975.

Schelling, T. C. *The Strategy of Conflict.* New York: Oxford University Press, 1960.

Schein, Edgar. *Process Consultation.* Reading, Mass.: Addison-Wesley, 1969.

Schon, Donald. *The Reflective Practitioner.* New York: Basic Books, 1984.

Sebenius, James K. *Negotiating the Law of the Sea: Lessons in the Art and Science of Reaching Agreement.* Cambridge, Mass.: Harvard University Press, 1982.

Simkin, William. *Mediation and the Dynamics of Collective Bargaining.* Washington, D.C.: Bureau of National Affairs, 1971.

Susskind, Lawrence E., and Michael Wheeler, eds. *Resolving Environmental Regulatory Disputes.* Cambridge, Mass.: Schenkman, 1983.

Talbot, Allan. *Settling Things: Six Case Studies in Environmental Mediation.* Washington, D.C.: The Conservation Foundation, 1983.

Walton, Richard E. *Interpersonal Peacemaking: Confrontations and Third Party Consultation.* Reading, Mass.: Addison-Wesley, 1969.

Wehr, Paul. *Conflict Regulation.* Boulder, Colo.: Westview Press, 1979.

Zartman, I. William, ed. *The Negotiations Process: Theories and Applications.* Beverly Hills: Sage Publications, 1975.

Zartman, I. William, and Maureen Berman. *The Practical Negotiator.* New Haven: Yale University Press, 1982.

Articles and Other Sources

Archibald, K. A. "Three Views of the Experts Role in Policy Making." *Policy Sciences,* 1970, pp. 73–86.

Bellman, Howard, Gerald Cormick, and Cynthia Simpson. "Using Mediation When Siting Hazardous Waste Management Facilities." (Washington, D.C.: Government Printing Office), July 1982.

Bellman, Howard, et al. "Environmental Conflict Resolution: Practitioners' Perspective of an Emerging Field." *Resolve* (Washington, D.C.: The Conservation Foundation), Winter 1981.

Center for Environmental Problem Solving (ACCORD). "Workshop Summary." Florissant, Co.: Environmental Conflict Management Practitioners' Workshop, October 1982.

Code of Virginia, Sec. 15.1 945.3 *et. seq.* (Statutes proscribing the duties of the Virginia Commission on Local Government, including its mediation role).

Colosi, Thomas. "Negotiation in the Public and Private Sectors: A Core Model." *American Behavioral Scientist,* 27:2, November 1983, pp. 229–253.

Cormick, Gerald W. "Intervention and self-determination in environmental disputes: a mediator's perspective." *Resolve* (Washington, D.C.: The Conservation Foundation), Winter 1982.

Cormick, Gerald W., and Leah K. Patton. "Environmental Mediation: Defining the Process Through Experience." (Seattle: Office of Environmental Mediation, Institute for Environmental Studies, University of Washington), February 1981, p. 28.

Fuller, Lon. "Mediation: Its Forms and Functions." *Southern California Law Review* 44: 305, 1971.

Johnston, Roger W. "Negotiation Strategies: Different Strokes for Different Folks." *Personnel*, 1982, pp. 36–44.

Kennedy, W.J.D., and H. Lansford. "The Metropolitan Water Roundtable: Resource Allocation Through Conflict Management" *Environmental Impact Assessment Review* (New York: Plenum) 4:1, 1983, pp. 67–78.

Klimoski, R. J. "The Effects of Intragroup Forces On Intergroup Conflict Resolution." *Organization Behavior and Human Performance* 8, pp. 363–383.

Harter, Philip J. "Negotiating Regulations: A Cure for the Malaise." *Georgetown Law Journal.* 71:1, 1981, pp. 1–118.

Lax, David A., and James K. Sebenius. "The Power of Alternatives or the Limits to Negotiation." *Negotiation Journal*, 1:2, April 1985, pp. 163–179.

Nicolau, George, and Gerald Cormick. "Community Disputes and the Resolution of Conflict: Another View." *Arbitration Journal*, 27:2, June 1982, pp. 98–112.

Richman, Roger. "Formal Mediation in Intergovernmental Disputes: Municipal Annexation Negotiations in Virginia." *Public Administration Review* (Washington, D.C.: American Society for Public Administration), 45:4, August/September, 1985, pp. 510–517.

——— . "Mediation in a City-County Annexation Dispute: The Negotiations Process." *Environmental Impact Assessment Review* (New York: Plenum), 4:1, March 1983, pp. 55–66.

——— . "Structuring interjurisdictional Negotiation: Virginia's Use of mediation in annexation disputes." *Resolve* (Washington, D.C.: The Conservation Foundation), Summer 1983, pp. 1, 4, 5.

Salem, Richard. "Community Dispute Resolution Through Outside Intervention." (Washington, D.C.: Society of Professionals in Dispute Resolution, Occasional Paper), 1982.

Saunders, Harold H. "We Need a Larger Theory of Negotiation: The Importance of Pre-negotiating Phases." *Negotiation Journal* (New York: Plenum), 1:3, July 1985, pp. 249–262.

Susskind, Lawrence. "Environmental Mediation and the Accountability Problem." *Vermont Law Review* 6, Spring 1981, pp. 1–47.

Susskind, Lawrence, and Jeffery Rubin, eds. "Negotiation: Behavioral Perspectives." Special Issue of *American Behavioral Scientist*, 27:2, November/December, 1983, pp. 131–279.

Virginia Commission on Local Government. *Report on the City of Fredericksburg-County of Spotsylvania Annexation and Immunity Agreement* (Richmond: Commission on Local Government), June 1982.

——— . *Report on the Town of Leesburg–County of Loudoun Annexation Agreement.* (Richmond: Commission on Local Government), March 1983.

Virginia House of Delegates. *Report on the Commission on City-County Relationships.* House Document No. 27, General Assembly Session, 1975.